Dr Melissa Starling holds a PhD in dog behaviour, personality, emotions and cognition. The self-styled Creature Teacher, Melissa works as a dog trainer and behaviourist in Sydney.

Professor Paul McGreevy is one of only three veterinarians recognised worldwide by the Royal College of Veterinary Surgeons as specialists in veterinary behavioural medicine. He is an animal behaviour and welfare expert at Sydney University's Faculty of Veterinary Science.

Dr Melissa Starling
& Prof Paul McGreevy

MAKING DOGS HAPPY

MURDOCH BOOKS
SYDNEY · LONDON

CONTENTS

INTRODUCTION

Making Dogs Happy is an informal look at the science behind making our canine pals as happy as they make us. We have referred to scientific research wherever it is relevant and available (references to our research are on page 256).

It is difficult to refer to what dogs, as a collective, like and dislike and how they behave. Just like humans, dogs have their own personalities and learned preferences, so they can differ dramatically in how they approach life and what they take from it. Any researcher who has worked with animals knows that whenever we think we understand the way they behave, there will be individual animals who buck the trend; individuals who did not read our textbooks and who are marching to the beat of their own drum. We have tried to address this wide range of variables in *Making Dogs Happy* by providing information on how to observe and understand dog body language and behaviour. This is one of the cornerstones of what we call 'dogmanship' and will allow readers to ask of their own dog: 'How relevant is this to you?'

We have suggested ways to test assumptions about the reasons our dogs do what they do, because it is always worth asking ourselves: 'How can I tell if I'm right?' Flexibility in our behaviour with dogs, and accepting that there might be a better approach than the one we like most, are hallmarks of good dogmanship.

We hope this book will empower dog owners to appreciate what their dogs might be feeling from moment to moment, and have strategies ready to respond in ways that support their dogs. Not only does this help head off problem behaviour in dogs, but it also fosters a rich and fulfilling human–dog relationship. We mention our free app, *doglogbook*, on several occasions when we see particular merit in monitoring and recording your dog's behaviour. Veterinarians around the world are asking owners to use *doglogbook* to collect data on behaviour of clinical importance. You can download the app at www.doglogbook.com.

We have threaded stories from our own experiences of living with dogs throughout the book to provide examples and to share some of our own joy. We are not perfect dog owners, nor are our dogs perfect. Embracing the ways they can both surprise and vex us is part of enjoying the unique aspects of sharing your life with another species.

You will get to know our own dogs a little bit through these pages. (Not enough to fall in love with them — because if you knew the full scope of their delightful personalities you would surely want them for yourselves and then they would be celebrities and people would stop us in the street to take selfies with our dogs.)

This book also features photographs that illustrate aspects of dog behaviour and human–dog interactions and how to interpret them. There is a good deal of information and scientific research we would have loved to share in more detail, but this is not a comprehensive text. *Making Dogs Happy* is focused on the practical application of current theory to improve your relationship with your dog and, of course, in the process to make your dog happy.

The following pages feature a rundown of the humans and dogs involved in the writing of this book. We urge you to dive in and embrace our scientist/dog-lover hybridised approach to making dogs happy.

Melissa and Paul

THE PLAYERS

DR MELISSA STARLING

Terminally curious and passionate animal lover Melissa knows that watching animals behave is like being invited into their world for a few moments. It is wondrous, fascinating and always raises questions. Melissa discovered in early high school that it is possible to make a career out of this. At university, studying zoology, it became apparent to her that no matter how much is learned about animal behaviour, it continues to be an exciting puzzle with only some of the pieces present. She hopes to be puzzled for the rest of her life.

KIVI TARRO

Nine-year-old Finnish lapphund and probably the best dog in the world, occasional social genius, regular comedian, frequent slightly animated floor rug and casual religious figure, Kivi is a very easy dog to live with and hard to imagine life without.

ERIK THE TALL

Middle-aged Swedish vallhund Erik is the TAGS (Talented And Gifted Student) dog, who finds mischief wherever he goes. The smartest dog we know, Erik is quirky, highly alert, optimistic, always on the lookout for opportunity and apparently obsessed with cause and effect. He likes his world arranged just so and has spent years studying doors – in particular, which doors should be opened and which kept closed.

KESTREL

Young Portuguese podengo pequeno Kestrel is a tiny hound and at times a spitfire. She is fond of vertical space, running very fast, swallows, novel environments, cuddles and embracing a healthy Mediterranean diet. She could be part-weasel. She is exceptionally good at inventing new games for humans to play with her; however, human cooperation is encouraged, but not required.

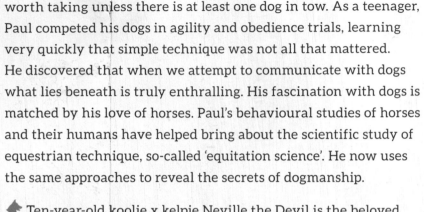

PROF PAUL McGREEVY

For veterinarian and animal watcher Paul, a walk is hardly worth taking unless there is at least one dog in tow. As a teenager, Paul competed his dogs in agility and obedience trials, learning very quickly that simple technique was not all that mattered. He discovered that when we attempt to communicate with dogs what lies beneath is truly enthralling. His fascination with dogs is matched by his love of horses. Paul's behavioural studies of horses and their humans have helped bring about the scientific study of equestrian technique, so-called 'equitation science'. He now uses the same approaches to reveal the secrets of dogmanship.

NEVILLE

Ten-year-old koolie x kelpie Neville the Devil is the beloved son of Wally (Paul's famous TV dog) and Tinker (below). When not accompanying Paul on twice-daily checks of their horse farm, Nev athletically and enthusiastically protects the resident chicken flock from marauding foxes, goannas and wedge-tailed eagles, and his burgeoning beef-bone collection from marauding Labradors.

BUNDY

Three-year-old Labrador retriever and former assistance dog Captain Bundy has been voted the boofiest and most affable dog in the history of dogkind. His enthusiasm for food and life (in that order) are legendary but led to trouble in his previous career. Dietary indiscretions, leading to two abdominal surgeries, forced an early retirement. But on the upside it earned him a new life in the country, where there is sufficient space for his need to assist with almost every human activity.

TINKER

Sadly, fun-sized working kelpie x koolie Tinker passed away during the writing of this book. She is missed chiefly for her charm and guile and the lessons in dogmanship she taught those around her who were prepared to learn. Her ability to spot snakes, avoid areas where she had seen them and raise the alarm when others were unaware was quite remarkable. Her dislike of snakes was eclipsed by her love of children.

1

WHAT MAKES A DOG HAPPY?

DOGS DON'T VALUE THE SAME THINGS AS HUMANS.

This is a relief for practical reasons — it is easier to be friendly with a being you are not competing with — but also for reasons of aesthetics. Imagine if we decorated our houses with a dog's sensibilities, for example. What would that look like? Understanding what dogs value is an excellent place to start understanding how to make them happy. So what do dogs value?

It pays to spend a little time thinking about the many ways in which a dog's world is very different to ours. Not only are their sense capabilities different, but also the way they process what they sense. Both sensing and processing are also likely to differ across breeds. Understanding how the world looks to a dog requires us to first acknowledge that your dog probably wouldn't even use the word 'look'. Humans are very preoccupied with vision because it is our most highly developed sense and so gives us the most information. Dogs are generally more interested in smell, and for good reason.

Stop and smell the single particle in a trillion

The power of a dog's nose and their ability to discriminate between odours is mind-boggling. A dog's sense of smell can be 10,000 to 100,000 times stronger than that of humans, depending on the breed.

'Smell you later!' A dog's world revolves around scent.

It seems that dog noses can be put to almost any sniffing task we can imagine. There are now dogs that can find such unlikely items as whale poo, mobile phones, dead bodies under seven metres (23 feet) of water and mud, and cancer cells and elevated cortisol levels in humans. Human consciousness of the world of scent is perhaps limited by our comparatively weak ability: dogs can sniff out scents we can't even imagine.

The odour-centric nature of a dog's world has a strong impact on his social life as well. Dogs detect chemical signals from one another using scent. Something called the vomeronasal organ detects chemical signals known as pheromones. Pheromones' signals relate to territorial and sexual behaviour, as well as to the mother–infant bond. The vomeronasal organ is located in the roof of the mouth behind the upper incisors, and dogs can feed odour molecules into it by flicking the tip of their tongue in and out of the mouth.

The main vehicle for pheromones is urine, but they are also secreted by the anal sac onto faeces as dogs defecate. So if you ever wondered why dogs seem completely obsessed with other dogs' urine, faeces and parts of the body where they come from, this is why. Just as we can look at another human being and see their age, gender, perhaps some hint of their health and success by what they look like and how they move or dress, dogs are thought to use pheromones to tell the age, sex, reproductive status and perhaps kinship and genetic differences of other dogs.

Dogs, just like us, are collecting information about who is around and how relevant they might be.

KIVI - ROLLING IN A GOOD STINK

One of the joys of being a dog owner is boasting about the most revolting item your dog has rolled in (that you have subsequently had to wash off them urgently). Melissa's Finnish lapphund, Kivi Tarro, is an expert at finding objectionable smells to roll in and it is evidently one of his favourite things to do. The most foul-smelling (to humans) perfumes he favours are fox faeces or rotting possum. Paul's Tinker concurred on the fox front but preferred foetid frogs to putrefying possums. There are many suggestions for why dogs roll in smelly things. Pat Goodmann at Wolf Park, a non-profit education and research facility in the USA, has reportedly revealed that wolves will roll in any unusual scent and that other wolves will follow the scent back to its source, supporting the notion that this is a way to bring information back to the pack. It has also been suggested that perhaps they use these scents in the way humans use perfume. It may be enlightening to look at where dogs like to 'wear' their perfume. The typical way for a dog to transfer a scent onto their body is to drop a shoulder and try to rub their neck and shoulder in the scent. Kivi has risked much in the past to get smears of decomposing possum, discovered on a steep incline, high on his neck ruff when it would have been a lot less perilous to just sit or maybe even lie on it or plant his face in it. This suggests that it matters to dogs where they carry this scent, but it is difficult to extrapolate why. Do they want it near their own nose, or near the noses of other dogs? Scent rolling is a behaviour that varies in dogs. Indeed, our own research shows that

continued...

it is more common in shorter dogs (perhaps because they are closer to the ground and the odours are more accessible to them) and in desexed more than entire dogs. Some dogs roll in stinky materials at any opportunity (Kivi), while others are only enticed to anoint themselves with the odd scent (Erik), and others seem to roll in anything remotely interesting whether it smells strongly or not (Kestrel considers a speck of pigeon faeces sufficiently interesting to take it home with her on her neck). If wild canids such as wolves do it more reliably than domestic dogs, that might hint at it being a residual behaviour from the dog's ancestry that doesn't serve a very important purpose anymore, but it has persisted in domestic dogs for so long that we must assume it serves them some purpose. So, we remain speculative about why dogs do this, and the jury is still out.

Kivi's top two best all-time lucky finds when it comes to interesting stinky things are to date: #2 a dead baby dolphin; and #1 a very much alive adult fur seal. Fortunately, Kivi has a good recall (comes when called) and was persuaded to refrain from rolling in the live seal, and smartly leashed for his safety and the seal's welfare. Although he was obviously quite entranced and kept drifting back zombie-like towards the exotic promises of a salty sea dog.

Rolling may release smells from the ground
and also allow dogs to leave their own.

What can dogs see?

Dog vision is not nearly as good as ours. They can see colour, static shapes and details, but dog vision is tailored for different uses to ours. Dogs are good at detecting movement and may be able to see a human arm waving up to a mile away. (You can verify this, should you ever find yourself in a quiet, flat, open area 1.5 km/1 mile long with minimal competing distractions.) For a more likely test, try training your dog to run to you when you wave your arm. A sound, as well, is helpful to get your dog's initial attention, but see how well the wave works on its own. Dogs are particularly sensitive to sudden or unusual movement — a sensitivity that primes them for detecting potential prey and that humans have taken advantage of for retrieving, herding and guide dogs. Dogs can see a little further than humans in a horizontal plane around them (250–270 degrees in dogs, versus 200–220 degrees in humans). Binocular vision is the ability of both eyes to work together to help with depth perception and this varies surprisingly in dogs, depending on the shape of the animal's head. Broad-skulled breeds, such as Pekinese or bull terriers, have slightly more binocular vision than narrow-skulled breeds such as greyhounds.

Dogs are not, as is sometimes claimed, completely colour blind. They can detect many of the same colours as humans, but they are essentially red/green colour blind. They see blue and greenish–yellow and yellow, but can't detect reds and oranges. However, they are better at detecting different shades of grey than are humans and they can see more detail at night, as they need less light than we do.

Do dogs hear what we hear?

Dog hearing is better than human hearing, but not within the same ratio as their superior sense of smell. Dogs can hear higher frequency sounds (35–65+ KHz) than humans (20 KHz for children). High-frequency sounds are abundant in nature, but probably the most important high-frequency sounds for a dog are the noises used for communication by small animals, such as rodents and bats. You can make a high-frequency sound by quickly gliding your thumb across the fingertips on the same hand. To humans, this sounds like a whisper of skin against skin, but to animals that hear higher frequencies it sounds like a squeak. Try doing this while your dog is napping lightly and look for ear twitches that might indicate they can hear the sound.

A NOTE ON SILENT DOG WHISTLES

'Silent' or high-frequency dog whistles are easily found in pet stores, but, like any whistle, they are unlikely to be meaningful just because the dog can hear them. And, as high-frequency sounds are more susceptible to degradation over distance — particularly in forested environments — a high-frequency whistle might not be a good choice for recalling a dog at a distance. Products are also marketed as 'dog silencers' — these are supposed to deter a dog from barking by emitting a high-frequency sound when the dog does so. The devices do not usually specify the KHz and dB (frequency and loudness) emitted, so it is difficult to know what the dog perceives when they are in use. In addition, the frequency of the sound is unlikely to be unpleasant to dogs, especially if we assume they evolved to hear in that range to help them find food. However, the loudness of the sound is another story. Dogs are well known for being frightened by very loud noises, such as gunshots, fireworks and thunder. It is highly likely that an effective dog silencer is emitting a very powerful sound that humans can't hear but dogs can. Any claims that such devices are humane should be met with caution; a dog's hearing can be damaged by very loud noises.

Sensitivity of dog skin

We might imagine that a dog's layer of fur dampens their sensitivity to touch. The fur is likely to be protective against cold, rough vegetation and terrain, and perhaps heat to some extent. Wild canid species, such as wolves, coyotes and dingoes, have a short-to-medium double coat with a soft undercoat for insulation close to the skin and an outer coat of guard hairs; this pattern is prevalent in many working-dog breeds. Coats in other dog breeds have become a matter of fashion, so it pays to be cautious about assuming all dog coats have a function related to improved performance or survival. Nonetheless, breeds developed in colder climates typically have denser, longer coats than breeds developed in more varied climates, and breeds developed in warm climates or for short bursts of intense, heat-generating activity might have only a short, single coat. But there are always exceptions, suggesting dogs in general can adapt to their local climate quite well.

Dogs' feet and noses lack a protective covering of fur, but seem less sensitive than human hands. They are tough and thick to provide some protection against injury during play, fighting, exploration and, in the case of the leather on a dog's feet, the usual hazards found on the ground that drive humans to a fondness for shoes. It is reasonable to expect that exposed parts of dogs are typically less sensitive to touch than human skin. This again reflects what our separate species have evolved to be good at. Human tactile abilities help us to grasp and move objects with precision and find small items by feel with our fingertips. Dogs don't have the appendages for such activities, but neither do they usually need clothes for warmth and protection. Their ability to dig through rough earth with no apparent discomfort seems to confirm that dog paws benefit from a lack of great sensitivity.

Fur protects a dog's skin from harsh physical stimuli. The nose lacks that protective covering.

Dogs do have one area that seems particularly tactile, and that is the muzzle. Whiskers are mobile and their structure amplifies movement to the point where just brushing gently past whiskers causes the dog's face to twitch. See if you can get a reaction from your dog without even touching him. We are unsure at this point how whiskers help dogs navigate their world, but it is likely they help dogs know how close objects (including other dogs, during play) are moving so they can respond accordingly — either to avoid a potential injury to fragile and critical parts of their bodies, such as their eyes, or to prevent the escape of prey.

Do dogs care about taste?

The expression to 'wolf down', meaning to eat big chunks of food hastily, evokes a familiar mental image for many dog owners. Most dogs tend to eat so fast that it is hard to imagine taste is important to them. Likewise, they appear to find an enormous range of organic materials worthy of a taste test, and many unlikely items to be palatable (see list opposite). They do tend to have preferences, though, and it is fun to find out what foods excite them. Most dogs favour meat and dairy products, for example.

Dogs usually sample unfamiliar potential food items with licks. Some dog owners may see this behaviour in their dogs at mealtimes if they have a fussy eater. To humans, who typically eat three meals a day, it can be worrying if their dog skips a meal — and this can result in human carers offering more palatable food, or offering it by hand. This might be enough to inadvertently train a dog to display reluctance to eat, which can lead to a narrow diet of acceptable foods in the long term.

SOME ITEMS THE AUTHORS' DOGS HAVE EATEN	SOME ITEMS THE AUTHORS' DOGS WILL NOT EAT
Fruits	Mushrooms
Raw vegetables	Iceberg lettuce
Used tissues	Leaves of most woody shrubs or trees
Faeces (any and all encountered)	Inorganic materials
Vomitus (any and all encountered)	Rocks
Unidentifiable putrid organic material	
Fish bait complete with maggots (it did not stay down)	
Animal carcasses (preferably old enough to smell objectionable to humans)	
Sand/soil	
Dried bluebottle stinging jellyfish	
Stones from apricots or peaches	
Corn starch packing peanuts	
Dry seaweed	
Flies, grasshoppers, cicadas, crickets	
Yoghurt, cheese, milk, raw eggs	
Bread, crackers, chips	
Raw fish, chicken, beef, pork, lamb, kangaroo meat and bones	

Dogs might not prioritise taste when eating, but male dogs do use it to monitor the sexual receptivity of female dogs and will lick the female's ears, lips and genitals during courtship. Lips and ears are touched to test the female's tolerance rather than to taste her, but licking genitals assists the male dog in detecting the female's hormonal status and, therefore, readiness to mate.

Dogs are good at details, but not the big picture

The human is a peculiar animal with an ability to form general rules very quickly. A dog is, like most other animals, a specialist in detail. To make a very human generalisation, dogs are not nearly as good as we are at generalising. We don't even remember learning that a black hatchback car and a white van are both types of vehicle, or that a vehicle can move fast or at walking pace or be stationary. We find it so easy to accept that someone can be in the driving seat of a moving car or a stationary car with the engine running, or a stationary car with the engine off, or standing by a stationary car with the engine running or the engine off, that it can be incomprehensible to us why a dog can apparently accept all these conditions for their owner's car, but suddenly get suspicious about a neighbour leaving their car running in the driveway while they run back into the house. To a dog, this is a completely different scenario to their owner leaving the car running in the driveway while they run back into the house.

Particularly alert and proactive dogs are liable to announce to the neighbourhood at large that their neighbour's car is doing something different. The neighbourhood is unlikely to appreciate this public service announcement, but these sorts of dogs do at least make very good watchdogs.

ERIK'S RULEBOOK

Erik the Swedish vallhund is a highly alert and proactive dog. This means he notices almost everything going on around him and generally defaults to assuming there's something he should be actively doing about it, unless he has learned otherwise. Melissa jokes that he has a rulebook in his head and every stimulus, scenario or event is checked carefully against the relevant entry, to assess whether he should issue a warning or just quietly update his rulebook. As a young and inexperienced dog, Erik's rulebook was thin; many stimuli were not in there, so he would often sound a strident rulebook-violation alarm. He gained more experience as he grew older, and added extra information to his rulebook to incorporate uncommon variations, such as 'the river actually CAN have small waves sometimes'. Conversely, the more similar experiences Erik collects about a particular context, the harder he finds it to accept small deviations. For example, he often visits a spot on the river near his home; and he often sees cormorants. But a cormorant on that particular spot on the river was unheard of for the first six years of Erik's life and he was alarmed to discover this bizarre combination of stimuli. On the other hand, an adult human wearing scuba diving gear warranted close examination on first encounter, but was more easily accepted. Humans wear a lot of different clothes, and Erik was not in familiar surroundings at the time. Perhaps he was more flexible with his rules in this context.

Of course Erik doesn't have an actual rulebook as such, but the metaphor does nicely describe how dogs build an understanding of their world through the accumulation of detailed and specific experiences, rather than the general patterns we humans use. This is why socialisation is so important for dogs. They are most mentally flexible as young animals, so exposing them gently to many stimuli with lots of minor variations not only helps them build their rulebook of what's normal in the world, entry by entry, but it also helps them build the skills to process and correctly assess novel experiences throughout their life.

Putting it all together

There are many ways in which dogs' appreciation of the world differs from ours; we receive and process information differently. This adds to the wonder of being around dogs, but it should remind us that we must never assume they are aware of the same stimuli that we are. Similarly, we may be unaware of what matters most to them. Only when we are aware can we take a walk in their paws and understand how to make them happy.

A walk through the park with a dog is a very different experience for the dog than it is for the human on the other end of the leash. The dog senses a world full of complex scents that contain information about who has passed here and when, what has been fossicking nearby and what humans have left lying around that might be edible. You stop to admire an intricately patterned insect with iridescent colours; your dog stops to admire a tussock of grass with layers of scent that may be every bit as fascinating to them. You see an acquaintance and stop to ask how they are; your dog does the canine equivalent by

*Dog greetings can be intimate affairs
when scent is so important.*

sniffing their dog's muzzle, then genitals and anus. Your dog sniffs around and lifts his leg on a shrub; the other dog gets precariously close to a damp head in her effort to get in and read the pee-mail. You notice bright birds with melodious songs; your dog stops and stares — ears up, tail stiff — at someone doing star jumps on a field several hundred metres away. Several streets away an ice-cream van starts playing music that your dog seems to think is the sound of the Gates of Hell being opened. You coach him through it until the sound dwindles, then it's time to throw a ball repeatedly so your dog can bring it back to you for the sheer joy of chasing it when you throw it away again.

They vex us at times, but the different ways that dogs perceive the world is part of what makes them such great company. Their simple joy in life puts a smile on our faces. More of that, please.

A dog's world is very different to ours,
but we share an interest in exploring it.

2

WHAT DOGS WANT ...

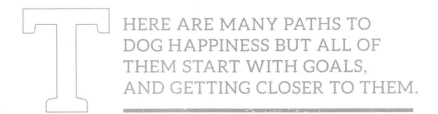

HERE ARE MANY PATHS TO DOG HAPPINESS BUT ALL OF THEM START WITH GOALS, AND GETTING CLOSER TO THEM.

Scientists working on rewards and emotions are beginning to suggest a simple, binary nature to positive and negative emotional states and how animals navigate their world to find rewards and avoid discomfort. They suggest that positive emotional states are inherently tied to getting closer to obtaining goals, while negative emotional states are inherently tied to getting further away from obtaining goals. For the sake of a dog-focused example, any time a dog is awake the world holds opportunities and there are a variety of goals the dog will find attractive. These goals depend on both the dog's current biological needs and the outcomes that become likely from moment to moment. The best dog owners are well aware of this and monitor their dog closely for patterns of behaviour that will tell them what is important to their dog. This is an example of dogmanship and explains why, regardless of whether they ever intended to be, these owners are lifelong students of dog behaviour.

Happy dogs are those that can chase their goals.

It's a dog's life, goal by goal

A dog's goals can vary wildly, just as human goals can. Let's take, for example, a dog in a multi-dog household, who is fed and walked in the morning. It is easy to imagine how her emotional state can change in just a few hours. We can map that out in a simple diagram that follows her goals and whether or not they are achieved (see opposite).

When it is approaching lunchtime and the dog is well fed, she has spent the early part of the morning (when she is most active) playing, running and exploring, she has relieved herself and no one in the household is doing anything of particular interest, her primary goal might be to simply rest comfortably. This is easily achieved and so she is content.

Perhaps she chooses to rest where she can monitor the household and be instantly aware of any interesting activity the moment it begins, such as her human heading to the bathroom. In that instant, her goal might switch from resting to trying to reach the bathroom door before it closes, so she can participate in bathroom-visiting with her human; her emotional state shifts, depending on whether she is successful or not. Maybe her human stood up from a desk because it's lunchtime, and when the human starts to move about the kitchen, her goal splits between participating in human activities in the kitchen and obtaining any food that falls onto the floor. Both these goals are easily met simultaneously by being in the kitchen.

Perhaps the sound of busyness in the kitchen entices another dog to come in, and now our first dog's goals split again to participating in human activities, obtaining any food that drops on the floor and maintaining a safe distance from the second dog to avoid being forcefully displaced from the kitchen. Imagine how both dogs' emotional states might fluctuate as they navigate this daily chain of events.

Dog follows
✓
POSITIVE

Human shuts dog out of bathroom
✗
NEGATIVE

Human gets up

RESTING
✓
POSITIVE

Human emerges
✓
POSITIVE

New dog arrives
✗
NEGATIVE

Watching for food
✓
POSITIVE

Human in kitchen
✓
POSITIVE

First dog manages distance to minimise conflict and maximise chances of obtaining dropped food
✗✓
(NEGATIVE/ POSITIVE)

Food drops
✓
POSITIVE

Dog beats other dog to food
✓
POSITIVE

Other dog displaces first dog in the kitchen
✗
NEGATIVE – BUT WORTH IT!

You can see that, at any one moment, our first dog is not necessarily happy or unhappy. She might or might not have achieved her goal, and it might be impossible to achieve all her goals without compromises. It might not even be clear if she is getting closer or further from her goal at any one moment. Some steps are ambiguous. In some households, going to the kitchen when food is being prepared is a fair bet (but not a sure bet) for snatching food off the floor. The arrival of the competitor dog introduces conflicting goals. Our original dog now has to weigh closeness to the potential food drop zone against the risk of aggressive behaviour from the other dog. Our first dog might move further away from the food preparation area, which means being further from the goal of obtaining fallen food, but closer to the goal of avoiding aggressive behaviour from the other dog.

So the first step towards making dogs happy is to identify their goals. Food, water, fun, company, safety and comfort seem to be important resources for dogs, regardless of breed or age, and obtaining resources is a common goal for all animals. However, dogs do have individual preferences that can be strong and, as we have just seen, what they want can change depending on time of day, degree of hunger, competing stimuli in the environment, their sense of safety and their energy level. One way we can identify a dog's goals is to use learning theory — in particular, instrumental conditioning.

LEARNING THEORY

Learning theory sounds terribly dull, but don't be put off by the name! It's a fairly simple framework that the best trainers apply all the time, even if they don't know they are doing so. It explains the mechanisms of animal learning and it applies to humans as much as to dogs.

Instant gratification

Early psychologists, such as Edward Thorndike and B. F. Skinner, discovered that animals are more likely to repeat behaviours that are immediately followed by a reward, such as food. The food therefore strengthens or reinforces the behaviour and can itself be called a 'reinforcer'. This kind of learning is generally called 'instrumental conditioning', because the response is instrumental in making the reinforcer appear (or in allowing the animal to avoid a noxious stimulus). Those who are familiar with psychology or animal training may be more familiar with the term 'operant conditioning', which is a term Skinner favoured to describe the trial-and-error learning that occurs when animals learn a new task by very simple problem-solving. The animal learns from the consequences of their attempts to acquire a reinforcer (reinforcement) or to avoid an unpleasant outcome (punishment). The signals that tell the animal when those consequences apply are known as 'antecedents'. For example, your dog might sit when you ask him to, but only when you have food in your hand. This is because the presence of food is the antecedent that tells him he will get food if he sits rather than you asking him to sit being the antecedent that tells him he will get food if he sits. This is a common training error. The solution is to ask him to sit when you don't have food in your hand, and then grab some from nearby (for example, your pocket) to give him when he does sit.

Understanding how rewards can reinforce behaviours is a powerful tool for identifying our dog's current goals. Whenever a dog starts performing a behaviour more often, with more intensity, or for longer, we can ask ourselves what is reinforcing this behaviour? What is the dog achieving with this behaviour? Be warned: the answer is not

Your dog might sit only when you have food, because the food is the best predictor of the dog being rewarded.

always obvious! In some cases, we can see a clear relationship ... Your dog rests his chin on your knee because you typically respond by stroking his head and fussing over how cute he is. He doesn't know that the combination of floppy cheeks and jowls over your knee and lifting his brows so he can gaze at you without moving his head is a near-lethal concoction of heart-melting adorableness that few dog-lovers can resist. He simply knows it leads to an affectionate human, and if he does more of it we can be sure that he enjoys the affectionate head stroking and fussing.

Using this framework, you can test your assumptions about your dog's preferences. If you suspect your dog likes something, start delivering it consistently and immediately after your dog has engaged in a particular behaviour. If the behaviour meets one or more of those criteria for being reinforced — it increases in frequency, duration or intensity — then you are spot on. This is a worthwhile exercise, because sometimes we are wrong about what our dogs like. Sometimes dogs have unintuitive ways of telling us when they don't like something (we will cover this in greater detail later) and not every dog follows the same patterns of behaviour. Sometimes the only way to decipher a dog's goal is to make a prediction and test it. Again, the best dog owners are lifelong students of dog behaviour.

WHEN A LICK IS A SHOVE

Most of the time when dogs lick us, it appears to be a sign of affection. Licking around the muzzles of other dogs is generally thought to be an appeasement or submissive behaviour that a dog will use to signal to another dog that they defer to them, and dogs might lick or nuzzle the same area when greeting a friend. However, some dogs — especially young dogs who are still gaining confidence in social situations — will lick another dog's, or a human's, mouth intensely as a way to strongly encourage them to move away without using any directly threatening signals. It is counter-intuitive, and a great example of a behaviour that benefits from testing to work out the reinforcer for that behaviour. Kestrel tries to lick between Kivi's teeth when he approaches one of the humans she is cuddling with. She growls if it's Erik approaching. It would be all too easy to assume she just likes Kivi better and is less threatened by him, until we note how each dog responds. Kivi tends to ignore snarling tiny hounds, but will not tolerate a tiny hound trying to climb into his mouth. He gives up and walks away. Erik would probably react violently to a tiny hound licking around in his mouth, but a growling tiny hound represents a confrontation he would rather avoid. Kestrel has evidently learned different strategies for holding her resources, depending on who is approaching them. Other dogs default to this obnoxiously frantic face-licking all the time. While it appears that the dogs involved are maintaining the peace and avoiding direct confrontation, this may be a brewing soup of conflict and suppression that can come to a boil over time. How long can Kestrel maintain her possession of human laps when the other two dogs would like a piece of thigh-pie as well? How long will the other dogs tolerate her unpleasant behaviour? An astute dog owner would step in and work to reduce the conflict and thereby enable all dogs access to the valued resource without aggravating each other, allowing the soup to cool.

Fortunately, dogs are expressive creatures and dog owners often have a good idea what their dogs like because of the way they respond to signals. Dogs that start to race around the house when someone says 'walk' are showing us with their enormous increase in unnecessary activity that they are very enthusiastic about what generally happens after someone says 'walk'. The decisions dogs make when two good things are available and they have to choose between them tells us about their preferences. The crinkle of a bag of treats being opened is often enough to convince a dog to come away from something they are barking at, whereas the promise of an ear scratch might not be enough to lure them.

Some reinforcers we prepared earlier

Every dog is an individual, which means we should not assume they all have the same reinforcers. Some dogs are intensely interested in interacting with humans, while others are expected to be aloof towards humans (e.g. many sight-hound breeds). The sight-hounds along with some small and delicate breeds (e.g. toy breeds) also tend to be sensitive rather than clumsy, so may prefer gentle interactions and dislike boisterous play. Nonetheless, there are some stimuli that are good bets as reinforcers for most dogs.

Food

Using food to reinforce dogs for desired behaviour often is a great way to encourage more desired behaviour, particularly with dogs that are on the independent side. When we want to let a dog know he has done really well, we can pay out big with a jackpot. Making the jackpot something novel and/or very tasty, or giving several pieces while

Anticipation of imminent reinforcers can be seen in the upright ears, steady gaze and relaxed, open mouth.

squealing about how clever, fabulous and bound for corporate success they are, can provide an exciting surprise for the dog, convincing them that what they just did was a stellar choice.

Dogs usually show general predictable preferences for different types of food that relate to their energy content or novelty. They usually prefer cheese over carrot, and roast meat over almost everything. There are always exceptions though, and we do well to 'ask the dog'. We can ask them by noting how eagerly they offer tricks they know can earn the treat on offer. Test one treat type per session to clearly see the differences. And remember to test each dog separately from any others, lest peer pressure leads to aberrant polling. Similarly, dogs will defend valuable resources and might even risk aggressive encounters in this pursuit. Neville and Bundy are great pals who often snooze, lounge and sleep up against one another but need plenty of space between them when fresh bones have their attention.

Water

Dog owners are rightly encouraged to provide drinking water at all times. Water is therefore often overlooked as a potential reinforcer, but drinking water is a resource that dogs definitely need to live.

Any thirsty animal will take risks to obtain water (this makes water sources a risky place to dwell for prey animals). Dogs could no doubt be trained to perform difficult and dangerous tasks for access to drinking water; however, that would first require them to be deprived of it. Deprivation is a proven method of increasing motivation to obtain a reinforcer, but may be morally questionable and can have direct health consequences, most notably kidney disease. Being a black dog in a hot climate, Bundy always makes the most of drinking water to cool down in summer, even if this means face-diving into the bowls that contain it and leaving them largely empty after impact.

Fun is the X-Factor

Humans value fun enormously, and it seems we are not the only ones. Fun is hard to define. While the dictionary simplifies it to enjoyment and amusement, the connotations are of playfulness and even purity of purpose. Fun is smiles and laughter, games and play. Dogs are undeniably a playful species. Unlike their ancestral counterparts, they play well into old age and many are not fussy about who they play with. Play is considered one of the few activities to be reliably and universally associated with a positive emotional state, so it is unsurprising that it can be a powerful reward for dogs; one they might prefer even over food. Yet, play is a concept that defies definition. It might be best defined by the emotional state of the performer.

Humans are not always good at identifying whether a dog is having fun or not, but there are signs that can be revealing. For example, a dog that keeps returning to an activity that is energetically costly with no obvious pay-offs, such as jumping on a bed or trampoline, running through piles of leaves, bounding through tall grass, or running ahead when they have guessed where the group is going, is showing that this activity is valuable to them. If no other reward is evident, other than the activity itself, then we must assume the dog finds the activity rewarding. A good example of activities with inbuilt rewards can be seen in herding dogs – they work for us not because they share our goal of moving livestock down a hillside and into a pen but because the very act of herding is rewarding in itself.

Some activities require effort to commence, such as climbing up a sand dune or a slide in a playground only to turn around and run, jump, or slide back down again. How instantaneously the dog dives into his descent and gets his pay-off can give us a clue as to how deliberate and pre-planned the action is. The dog might also indicate his enjoyment of an activity through his body language.

Dogs will invest a
lot of energy into
obtaining the goals
they desire.

Playful body language includes exaggerated movements of the head and limbs, unnecessarily energetic leaps and bounds, vocalisations such as barking and growling and, usually, a softness and looseness in the face and throughout the body. Dogs might have different preferences when it comes to playful signals. And dogs of different breeds have preferred play styles. For Paul, this was confirmed the first time he witnessed Bundy encountering a fellow Labrador retriever. The play bows, body wriggles and hindquarter bounces were articulated in fluent Labradorese. Kivi is one for tossing his head like a pony and running in big, exaggerated bounds, or flopping abruptly on the ground and barking until someone comes over to tickle or climb on him or (Erik!) bite his genitals. Erik is more intense and uses little growls and barks, but his tail wags are loose and his ears not as erect and forward-pointing as they would be if he were threatening another dog. To invite play, Bundy cavorts with his tail held almost as if it is chasing him. Meanwhile, Nev will ostentatiously pick up over-sized sticks, logs and even branches as if they are the most prized of all possessions only to then deliberately drop them in the path of other dogs. The muscles that move his lips and muzzle are also more relaxed, and when he makes contact with another dog he turns to one side at the last moment so that contact is largely made with the 'safe' parts of his body, including his flanks, hindquarters or shoulders.

A sense of humour?

It has not officially been established if dogs have a sense of humour, but they do use a vocalisation that has been dubbed a 'dog-laugh'. It has attracted this beguiling label because it occurs exclusively during play or friendly greetings. The dog-laugh sounds like a breathy, forced

Unhesitating and enthusiastic commitment to any activity suggest the dog enjoys it.

exhalation and dogs usually respond to it with playful behaviour and sometimes their own dog-laugh. It has recently been reported that playbacks of the dog-laugh reduce signs of stress and increase social, approach behaviours in shelter dogs. A human whispering to a dog, especially in an excited manner, can produce a similar response, so it's possible that dogs interpret pronounced, breathy exhalations from humans as a dog-laugh. Before you try this yourself with the next dog you encounter, it pays to be aware that breathing (or whistling) very close to a dog's face can annoy it.

If dogs did have a sense of humour, what kinds of things might they find funny? Perhaps looking at what makes human babies laugh can provide some ideas. Babies seem to be amused by nice, safe surprises, such as an object suddenly moving, disappearing and reappearing, making an interesting sound, or changing shape. Dogs find many surprises frightening, but surprises that are quite obviously safe tend to elicit playful body language. It is critical to ask the dog in front of you what they like, and that means looking for signs of conflict, which will be covered later in the book, and giving the dog many opportunities to end the interaction or retreat.

WHAT'S FUN FOR SOME IS NOT NECESSARILY FUN FOR ALL

Melissa occasionally takes her dogs along a walking trail with a very steep, narrow, somewhat rocky section. We can only guess how this idea coalesced, but one day Erik suddenly got busy attacking Kivi's legs and trying to push him down the steep trail. Kivi lost his footing and rolled over and over, out of control, for about 10 metres (33 ft) before he regained his feet. Apparently this tickled Erik, because he quickly developed a strategy that could topple Kivi in moments on that steep trail. The length of time between visits allowed Melissa to forget what had happened the previous time, but Erik did not. Every time he started down the trail, he would dart in and expertly attack Kivi's balance. Down Kivi would go, and Erik would stand there, watching him roll, and then run after him to try to do it again. Needless to say, Melissa eventually caught on and put a stop to this for Kivi's wellbeing and safety, but it remains a good example of what might be considered fun for a dog — probably the same kind of rough-house nonsense that is fun for young children. Like young children, dogs can also lack the mental ability to appreciate that fun with a friend requires both parties to be enjoying themselves, or that a fun activity could be dangerous.

It is important to note that 'fun' is not always just the activity itself. Dogs who typically lose games of possession often become less interested in those kinds of games and can take months to recover their confidence after a series of defeats. They might also become less interested in competing in other scenarios. Likewise, dogs that are bullied during play can become withdrawn around other dogs and even start to become aggressive towards them. When the fun goes out of an activity it can discourage dogs from seeking fun in places where they have found it before, and discourage them from seeking rewards in general. This risk-aversion — unwillingness to take risks — can be a manifestation of pessimism.

Evidence shows that animals kept in environments with few opportunities for enjoyable activities (often called 'enrichment') seem to expect fewer positive outcomes for themselves and more negative outcomes. Dogs that are reluctant to take risks might not find the sources of joy and reward that an optimistic, risk-taking dog can find. The less they find and acquire these rewards and positive experiences, the less they expect to find them, and the more risk averse they can become. Risk-averse dogs can be easy to live with in some ways — not as prone to look for fun and mischief — but training them might be a challenge if they are unwilling to try new behaviours. In contrast, an optimistic dog that expects more positive outcomes might be inclined to risk venturing further or tackling an obstacle to see what the environment has to offer. This can produce a dog who takes some work to manage off leash but is likely to be relaxed about offering new behaviours and exploring novel activities and environments. This is a dog that is easy to train and resilient to whatever life might throw at them; a dog that finds joy wherever it is available.

COGNITIVE BIAS

Melissa was lucky enough to study canine optimism as the core of her PhD. She trained dogs to expect good and neutral outcomes for responding to particular sound signals. Then she asked the dogs to respond to new tones — these tones fell somewhere between the sounds that led to reward and the sounds that led to disappointment (neutral). These studies of so-called cognitive bias, or judgment bias, are the most promising lead we have for what many animal welfare scientists regard as the Holy Grail in their field: being able to ask animals how they feel. There is growing evidence that measures of optimism decline in animals who experience reduced welfare. So shifts in their cognitive bias can potentially reveal shortfalls in an environment to which human observers are entirely oblivious.

Want to go for a W-A-L-K?

How many dog owners have to spell out 'the W word' rather than say it? When spoken in full, the word promises such good times that unwitting humans must withstand 30 kilograms (5 stone) of excited canine careering around the house. In Melissa's home we must be careful not to discuss where we might 'take the dogs' before there is an imminent plan. The question 'Who wants to go to the park?' is met with three intense, furry faces trying to force 'ME' into the speaker's brain via sheer willpower. At certain times of the day just closing the laptop or saying 'OK ...' can incite instant hopeful canine attention.

Why do dogs enjoy outings so much that they figure out a long list of clues as to when they might be about to depart on one? Why does the promise of virtually any outing excite most dogs? Outings provide opportunities for many enriching activities: sniffing, playing, peeing, pooing, exploring, eating from the smorgasbord nature provides, meet-and-greets, marking, sex (although, we hope not) — all activities that may not be readily available at home. Outings may be especially exciting for domestic dogs because, unlike their free-ranging brethren, their human family can take them to visit environments rich in stimuli that they don't encounter at home: forests, beaches, lakes, mud flats, rivers, picnic parks and dog parks, if the dog enjoys meeting canine strangers. It is remarkable that we can visit the same places over and over with a dog, yet the dog still conveys the same urgency to sniff, mark, run, roll and socialise as on every previous visit. The opportunity to engage in these activities is obviously highly valued by dogs, although some of them might baffle us humans. Why does Kivi sample the grass of seven different front lawns in 100 metres by flopping onto his back and rolling languorously this way and that? He has access to lawns at home and does not spend nearly as much of his time collapsing abruptly onto them. The relative disinterest in the

grass available at home is a good hint that it's not the grass exactly that is so enticing. In a world that is mostly smells, rolling might be a way for the dog to spread its odours for others to pick up, or to release odours held in the vegetation to collect information. Or maybe it's a tactile exploration of different grass varieties. Kivi seems to favour scratchy lawns, soft new turf and frosty grass. As tempting as it is to say he rolls more on grass when it's frosty because he's a Northern breed, a simpler explanation is more consistent with his preferences. Frosty grass is stiff and scratchy, too.

It's worth remembering and pondering on the ways dogs may find stimuli and activities inherently rewarding for reasons we might never truly understand. This can explain some of the troublesome behaviours dogs display as well. Sledding breeds, such as huskies, were bred to run and pull, so for them, running and pulling may be innately rewarding. Terriers might find hunting around in shrubs for small animals innately rewarding, while Border collies and other herding dogs like Neville, can find chasing moving objects innately rewarding. The herding dogs often work sheep independently of humans simply because they find the work of chasing so enjoyable. We should not be surprised that, in the absence of livestock, dogs of these breeds are high risk for chasing joggers, skateboarders, cyclists and even cars.

Outings also provide opportunities for physical exercise, especially stretching the legs and going for a run. Just as humans are built to enjoy running ('humans' in general — personal experience can vary!) a study has shown that dogs experience a 'runner's high' physiologically similar to the neurological rewards that make endurance or high-intensity running rewarding for humans. This is not experienced in dogs when they walk for long periods, but only after aerobic exercise.

The optimistic dog knows that outings provide many opportunities for enrichment and access to rewards.

Many dog breeds have historically had jobs that required long periods of intense activities. Most gundogs, herding breeds, some scenthounds, sledding breeds, some terriers and a few other active 'utility' breeds, such as Dalmatians and Boxers, were expected to be engaged in active pursuits for much of the day on a regular basis. Many dogs can adapt to less exercise than they might have been bred for or are used to, but we ignore their activity history at our peril. Under-exercised dogs can become restless, destructive, vocal, easily over-excited and pester us to play or take them out. These are not signs of a typically young and silly dog (or old and silly dog), but signs of chronic frustration. Selecting a dog breed with expected exercise requirements that fit comfortably within your current lifestyle is a great place to start. Of course, dogs don't always live up to expectations, and there are times when owners might need to accept that the best toy for a dog is another dog, especially one of the opposite sex. Dog parks and/or regular play dates with dogs that get along well can be good ways to take the edge off a dog's exercise needs. There are, of course, pitfalls with dog parks in particular and this will be addressed later in the book.

Man's best friend needs friends

Animals that have evolved to live in groups often seem to need some company. 'Need' is a strong word, suggesting that they will not thrive without it. There is little data to support that assertion, but it is being increasingly recognised by zoos and wildlife parks how important it is to house social species in groups that are structured similarly to how they live in the wild. Domestic dogs don't really have a 'wild' state that can be referred to. Studies show that 'free-ranging' dogs — dogs that

Some breeds, such as Dalmatians, were bred to be active. Such dogs may highly value physical exercise.

are free to move through the landscape and associate with whomever they want — often form pairs or groups, probably related to food availability. For example, village dogs that roam human habitations for food that is scarce and distributed over a wide area tend to do so alone or in pairs. Free-ranging dogs in areas where food is more centrally located and abundant, such as rubbish tips, form larger groups.

Given the adaptability of dogs, it would be fair to suggest their social structure defies definition. They can exist as loners, or in pairs, or in larger groups. The question becomes: do they prefer company if they have the freedom to choose it? This is a difficult question to ask dogs and subsequently a difficult question to answer, and it undoubtedly depends on the dog in question. Observing the amount of time a dog spends in the same room as company, and how close he chooses to be to that company given the space available to him, can be revealing. Many dogs seem particularly attracted to the social group. The living room in the evening, when adults and children may congregate, is the place the family dog often wants to be. And the dining table at mealtimes includes the added lure of possible food.

Many dogs will choose to share the sofa or a bed with other members of the family, even when we have provided them with appropriately sized, soft and padded furnishings of their own. This hints at the value dogs hold for resting close to or in contact with other family members, whether they are humans or other dogs.

Safety first

Dogs are motivated to seek out and obtain a variety of goals. These might include tangible rewards, such as food and water, or more conceptual goals, such as fun, company and social interactions, and safety. Any behaviour that is increasing in frequency, duration and/or intensity is almost certainly being reinforced. A reinforcer is a stimulus that is sufficiently rewarding that the animal will work to obtain more of it. This knowledge can help us identify what a dog values, and can also help us work out the dog's goals from one moment to the next. If in doubt, test your assumptions! If your dog truly does like something, you should be able to use it to reinforce a particular behaviour, such as *sit* or *touch*.

The most vital resource for a dog (and any other animal) is a sense of safety. (An exception might be the fun that some dogs, notably terriers, seem to think they can have with highly venomous snakes — although they probably don't appreciate how brave they are being.) Safety always comes first and this can be depended upon as a reinforcer. It is intriguing that humans should relate to this deeply and yet so often seem surprised when their dog won't do what they want because it's too busy trying to ensure its own safety to attend to trivial requests. Think of it this way: if you suspect an axe murderer is roaming the neighbourhood and might even be that person coming towards you, how motivated might you be to, say, sit down? Your friend next to you keeps grunting your name and telling you to *sit*. They get increasingly frustrated with you for not sitting down. They wave chocolate in front of your nose. You can't imagine why you would possibly want chocolate right now and, frankly, it's blocking your view of the possible axe murderer, who is now rapidly approaching. Your friend yells your name — you are vaguely aware of this through your intent focus on avoiding an ugly wedge of sharp metal in your back. Your friend tugs roughly on your clothes and it drags you off balance. Some friend! The axe murderer is almost upon you and they are getting in your way, yelling, waving chocolate around and yanking you off balance. You try to ignore them and lunge at the axe murderer in a desperate bid to protect yourself. This scene plays out for many dogs across the Western world on a daily basis. The axe murderer usually turns out, at worst, to be a somewhat unstable and belligerent social disaster of another dog, but he's on a leash and probably can't touch you as he passes within inches on the same footpath, so why worry? Think how worried you would be passing within inches of a 'safely' handcuffed axe murderer. Now think how worried you would be if, several times in the past, this had resulted in hair-raising moments when the axe murderer suddenly lunged and did manage to touch you.

Few other possible rewards are likely to hold much sway with a dog that does not feel safe. Safety is a pressing goal, although it can certainly feature in scenarios of conflicting goals, and we often see this with dogs that are lured to receive pats from strangers by the promise of food. They may approach for the food even if they dearly do not want to be patted. They become very ready to defend themselves, though. Some dogs (Erik) have an uncommon gift for multi-tasking that allows them to switch with enviable ease from one activity to another in an instant. Such dogs might continue to work for rewards, such as food, until the point where their sense of safety is deeply compromised. Other dogs respond with a strong withdrawal at relatively minor disturbances. A stranger touching their paw might be enough to convince them they have a lot going on right now and can't afford to do things like eat until it's all sorted out. And there are dogs all along the continuum between.

We do well to remember that safety always comes first with our dogs and other animals. There are several reasons a dog might not perform a behaviour they apparently know well, or even pay attention to their humans, and we will cover others later. But the first question should always be whether the dog feels safe.

Safety trumps all, and making our dogs feel secure with us should be a priority.

3

... AND WHAT DOGS DON'T WANT

**HERE IS A FLIP SIDE TO THE CONCEPT OF GOALS AND THEIR ASSOCIATION WITH POSITIVE EMOTIONAL STATES.**

We briefly explored safety as a most valued resource, and thus a reinforcer of behaviour, in the previous chapter. Obtaining safety is believed to be one route to positive emotional states, but the other side of this coin is that safety can be obtained by escaping or avoiding threats. Without threats, safety would be meaningless. It goes without saying that feeling threatened is not generally akin to feeling happy. Regardless of the indisputable merits of obtaining safety, repeated exposure to potential threats induces risk aversion. It follows, then, that in striving for happy dogs we should avoid exposing them to stimuli they find unpleasant enough to want to avoid or escape. Later we will focus in more detail on how to coach dogs through aversive (noxious, unpleasant) experiences. But first, let's focus on the kinds of stimuli and experiences that dogs dislike.

WHAT DOES A DOG IN PAIN OR DISCOMFORT LOOK LIKE?

The distinction between pain and discomfort is difficult to define in humans, let alone with non-verbal animals. Therefore, for the sake of simplicity, we will treat pain and discomfort as one. A dog has pain receptors all over its body, as does a human. These provide critical feedback that encourages a dog to move away from extremes of heat, cold and injury: they keep a dog safe. Signs of pain and discomfort can also tell us when a dog is injured or ill and when they are experiencing a sensation they dislike. Melissa knows that sometime in spring, 'prickle season' will start, when small weeds in grassy areas produce sharp seed cases that were the bane of every barefoot kid's existence during her childhood. Erik and Kivi walk very slowly across grass in prickle season, and Erik is particularly susceptible to freezing in the middle of a patch of prickles and waiting to be rescued. Tinker seemed able even to smell and thus avoid the plants that produced prickles. In contrast, Kestrel does not seem to notice them at all.

Melissa recently conducted an informal experiment with commercially available dog boots. They seemed to be well received by Erik, who ran across the prickly grass much more deftly than usual, and even stopped when he lost a boot and waited for it to be refitted. Kivi's response to boots, however, was to refuse to move or even eat, so evidently boots are even more unpleasant to Kivi than prickles. This illustrates how important it is to listen to our dogs by reading their behaviour and appreciating how their discomfort or pain manifests.

While pain and discomfort are universal to humans and dogs, remember that these sensations can vary broadly in intensity and in the way they are perceived by different dogs. What is painful to one dog may be barely noticed by another, so it pays to consider how a dog experiencing pain or discomfort would behave. According to social media comments, if cement or asphalt is too hot for a human hand, it is too hot for a dog's paw. We know that a dog's sense of touch might differ from ours: hot surfaces can burn paws, which is why sniffer dogs working a shift on hot surfaces are often fitted with protective boots. However, what would a dog do if her feet were uncomfortably hot? Would she show no signs of her discomfort, leaving it entirely up to our hands on the ground to determine if she was uncomfortable? Consider how she could alleviate her discomfort. She could take opportunities to walk on cooler surfaces such as grass. Or pick up her feet quickly to minimise contact with the hot ground, or hold up one or two paws to give them some relief, like lizards do in the desert. She might stand in the shade and show reluctance to leave it. Walking in unshaded places on a hot day is uncomfortable, even for people wearing shoes. Might signs of doggy discomfort relate to sensations other than hot paws? She might pant heavily, trying to cool herself down, or become lethargic as we do when it's hot. We might be better served by observing dogs for signs of distress or discomfort than by letting social media comments dictate to us when all dogs will be distressed.

Dogs can be jerks

Many dog owners discover their dogs are not very good sharers, in spite of efforts to instil this human value. Indeed, dogs are regularly selfish jerks when it comes to resources. Possession is a full 10 tenths of the law in dogland but dogs are not mean-spirited — they are simply highly opportunistic.

Dogs have evolved with unreliable access to many of the resources they value most. In a dog's world it pays to grab what you can, when you can, and attempt to hold onto it. Studies have shown that dogs have a distinctive growl specifically to deter other dogs approaching

Dogs are not always good sharers
of toys and other resources.

items in their possession. These possessions can include food, chew items, toys, resting places, sticks, balls, or even the dog's owner. The growling and grabbing are part of what is known as 'resource guarding', as the purpose of these behaviours is to guard a resource from potential competitors.

Traditionally, in ecology, a 'resource' is something necessary for an animal's growth, maintenance and reproduction, but this definition does not encompass everything the modern dog can feel compelled to try to protect from others. A toy is not strictly necessary for growth, maintenance and reproduction, but a dog might still be unwilling to allow other dogs near it.

It is unlikely that dogs enjoy defending their resources. Aggressive behaviour is often potentially costly in that it increases the risk of injury and can also jeopardise social harmony, which can lead in turn to an increase in unpleasant interactions. Resource guarding can manifest particularly in times of anxiety or distress. So it is worth considering a dog's willingness to engage in aggressive behaviour, particularly related to the resource in question, and the dog's current emotional state. If we find our dog is being unusually intolerant of other dogs coming near a resource, it could be time to ask if our dog's emotional state is unusually negative. Everyone has bad days, including dogs. However, if it becomes a trend it is worth investigating with a professional.

OWNERSHIP AND DEFENDING RESOURCES

Erik loves trick training. Melissa can tell, because he has learned many strategies to manipulate her into kicking off a trick-training session, including some that have seen him venture into outright delinquency. He also apparently 'owns' training cues. He does not tend to repel strange dogs from approaching his humans, regardless of whether they are carrying food or not. However, if a strange dog is hanging around when someone (anyone) gives him a cue for a trick that he knows, he does get agitated and is liable to try to drive away the unfamiliar, potential competitor. Is he defending the cue for a behaviour he enjoys, or is he defending the anticipated imminent arrival of treats, which often follow tricks? It may be academic in this case, but we can be assured that using tricks to move him away from a strange dog he does not appreciate is effective, but may exacerbate the situation if we are not careful to ensure the other dog doesn't follow.

When is a dog not a selfish jerk?

We expect many readers are now mentally citing all the times their dog has been generous or nurturing or seemed to show compassion. Recent studies show that dogs can indeed display what appears to be generosity. They will perform behaviour that results in a food treat going to another dog. The conditions under which this is likely to occur are: 1) the dog performs a behaviour to donate treats that he himself does not receive during the experiment; and 2) the dog that receives the treats lives with the 'donor' dog. Social animals are wondrous creatures with deliciously complex behaviours that help them live in harmony with other members of their species, who are also their closest competitors for valued resources. As such, many dogs behave differently towards dogs with whom they live or have a long-term relationship, compared to dogs they meet transiently (it pays to be less of a jerk towards individuals you are going to compete with on a daily

basis). Many (but not all!) dogs will adjust their behaviour over time to minimise aggressive interactions with canine housemates, while also maximising their own access to resources. The resulting compromise is one of dogs' marvellous socially acrobatic feats. We are still understanding what it means on a basic level to be a social non-human animal, but it does make sense to forge mutually positive social bonds, to be inherently attracted to familiar individuals, to be protective of one's social group, to pay attention to what interests others in the group and what they find threatening or alarming, and to behave in ways that minimise conflict with them.

Loss of control

We all know the comfort of being in control of our own destiny. Losing control of a situation can lead to feelings that range from mild anxiety to outright terror. We could argue that dogs value control over events, but this does not quite capture the way dogs learn to avoid situations they anticipate will rob them of control. Small dogs are frequently picked up and carried by humans, but what does this really mean to the dogs in question? It means they are no longer in control of where they go, what they can explore and what they can smell. They do not know how long this situation will persist; they have no ability to retreat if they are taken close to stimuli they are not comfortable with; and they are at the mercy of the person carrying them. It is astonishing that more small dogs don't learn to retreat or hide when a human reaches for them; it might be that they simply learn they are helpless to prevent this, and/or that being picked up is usually tolerable. There are always individuals who don't mind, or truly enjoy, being picked up and carried around, and these are the dogs that

Holding dogs reduces their sense of control.
Let them choose to be held.

actively present themselves to be picked up and show no evasion. This is why we really need to find ways to ask our dogs and give them the opportunity to answer with a definite 'yes' (approach/cooperation) or a 'no' (retreat/evasion). Our own studies have shown that small dogs are more inclined to show owner-directed aggression. The reasons are not clear, but one possible contributing factor could be how often their owners rob them of control by picking them up against their will.

Many grooming and husbandry practices we inflict on our dogs also rob them of control. There is no choice in being shampooed, or having your paw picked up and held while your toenails are clipped. There is no choice in being restrained while a vet checks your ears and teeth.

Take the time to ensure dogs are willingly entering into an activity — that could include giving them the chance to stop the activity at any time or to leave. Exceptional trainers reward animals for cooperating whenever they might not completely enjoy the activity. The dog is rewarded every time it is asked to participate and given jackpots for signs of relaxation and improved compliance. This also provides some buffering against accidents. If you always 'pay' your dog to cooperate with nail clipping, if you accidentally injure him once it is unlikely to have as profound an impact as if he had never been rewarded.

Miscommunication

Loss of autonomy can form a large component of a dog's goal to avoid a particular stimulus or activity, but its aversiveness can be amplified when that stimulus or activity starts out as confusing for the dog.

Our own research has identified that many human behaviours towards dogs have no equivalent in the dog–dog ethogram (the catalogue of behaviours and actions that amount to the canine social repertoire). This means that dogs have no frame of reference for activities such as veterinary examinations, baths, nail clipping, grooming, training with treats, towelling dry and walking on a leash. Some of these human behaviours to dogs could have conflicting interpretations, based on the dog–dog ethogram. For example, dogs do not often hug each other, but the nearest equivalent might be clasping to hump, or clasping the shoulders with the forelegs. Both of these behaviours can trigger aggressive responses in other dogs. It is unclear why exactly, but it might be that physical restraint in this fashion reduces a dog's ability to move away as she might wish to, so her sense of safety declines. Furthermore, dogs will pin other dogs forcefully to the ground in aggressive encounters, so she may be anticipating an aggressive manoeuvre. Similarly, we humans don't necessarily like being seized by someone unless we trust that person will release us when we ask. It is interesting that many humans expect dogs to accept physical restraint in all its forms and by anyone — stranger or familiar — as a matter of course. Why would they? They rarely accept it from another dog they don't trust explicitly. Typically, dogs are more amenable creatures with humans than they are with each other. Even if they show signs of distress, they will generally tolerate with good grace being restrained and handled in ways that do not usually feature in dog–dog interactions. Perhaps this tolerance has shaped human expectations of dog behaviour so that when a dog does object, with a warning growl or even a snap, it is seen as misbehaviour by the dog rather than the dog objecting to misbehaviour by the human.

Space invaders

Humans are prone to display the same behaviour to dogs that they usually reserve for children. Kissing puts a human face extremely close to a dog's face and many dogs find this uncomfortable, at least at first. When dogs touch each other's faces, it is usually least likely to provoke aggression when performed very slowly and gently so that the dog can move away if he finds the proximity troubling. Similarly, humans tend to lean over dogs to pat or talk to them. To a dog, this posture might resemble a dominating stand-over or a predatory crouch in preparation for grabbing, rather than a friendly overture.

Some dogs will jump up in response to this crowding and bop the human in the face with their nose. This is often interpreted as a friendly greeting by humans, but as always, testing the assumption can be revealing. A polite dog greeting involves often one or more pauses in approach to gauge the other dog's interest in a social interaction. Crouch down and encourage a dog to come to you. Do you still get bopped? Do you get bopped if you first rub the dog's head or face? What about if you greet her with hands on her flanks instead? You might start to see an emerging pattern that tells you the bop is probably a request for space rather than an affectionate kiss. (Of course, some dogs would live inside your skin with you if given the option, but it's good practice to ask the dog.)

The astute reader might notice a pattern forming in this section. Many of the behaviours we direct at dogs that they might find uncomfortable are those that invade their personal space. The dog, like any animal, has a personal space bubble, usually known as peri-personal space. This refers to the area immediately surrounding an animal's body. Peri-personal space is typically largest around the face, which makes good sense: the face is the site of vulnerable organs, such as the eyes and nose. And right behind the face is the brain, which must be kept very safe indeed. Injuries to these areas can be serious — even life threatening — so animals react in a self-protective manner to objects that enter this space. The speed at which an object is moving towards an animal dictates how strong the resulting evasive

A hand descending towards a dog's face can seem very threatening!

response will be ... there's nothing like a football flying at your face to get you a bit twitchy.

Humans do well to appreciate that dogs, and indeed all animals, prefer to have several escape routes when they are approached, particularly by a stranger, or when they encounter novel objects. A single escape route can very easily be blocked in a critical moment, e.g. by the approaching human. A dog might respond with an increase in the size of their personal space bubble, giving them the room and opportunity to react and escape if the potentially threatening object moves towards that one escape route. A dog with two escape routes has one extra choice, so can afford a smaller personal space bubble and a higher level of risk. And so it goes; a dog with three options for escape can afford a smaller personal space bubble and more risk-taking again. In this way, dogs that are approached while in a crate, a kennel, or on an armchair, for example, can feel that a head-on approach is blocking their only escape route. These are the dogs who are moved to increase the distance between themselves and an uninvited approach, perhaps by a veterinarian. They might resort to an overt warning, such as a growl, to tell the approaching individual to quit approaching or there will be trouble.

Added to the complexities of perceived escape routes and their relationship to risk-taking and personal space bubbles is the dog's perceived level of threat. The personal space bubble gets larger the more likely a dog judges that they will need to escape. For most dogs without an anxiety disorder, this is simply a game of numbers. The more times they need to escape, the more likely they judge they will need to in future. The more times they think they might need to escape and then don't, the less likely they judge they will need to escape in the future. They adjust their personal space bubble accordingly. This is powerful knowledge.

Repeated space invasions will train dogs to be more and more reactive to the possibility of this happening again. We see this sometimes with dogs that live with small children, who are able to move into their space and touch them, sometimes at any time, including when the dog is at rest or with food or toys. While some dogs are fabulously tolerant of this, many find it distressing. Neville is fascinated by children, most of whom are immediately drawn to him, possibly by the amazing colours in his coat, but he approaches them only when there is an assured escape route. For those dogs who cannot be assured peace from a wandering child, we are likely to see two key changes in behaviour. Firstly, they become more sensitive to children approaching. Their perceived level of threat when they are around small children increases, so their personal space bubble increases, which leads to even more space invasions as the child doesn't even need to make contact anymore to be a space invader. Secondly, the dog might begin to switch tactics from defence (escape) to offence. It should be stressed that a dog that growls or snaps at small children is not necessarily a mean dog. They simply could have learned that small children are incorrigible space invaders, and all polite requests for space are ignored. What choice do they have but to ask more forcefully? Whenever a dog is becoming more aggressive towards a particular trigger, such as children or other dogs, we should be suspicious of what the dog has been learning about this trigger's propensity to invade their space. How they do it can also be revealing. Some dogs can be tolerant and relatively friendly towards other dogs if they approach slowly, but might be outright offensive towards dogs that approach too quickly or exuberantly.

Knowing about the numbers game is also a powerful means of treating distance-increasing behaviours, such as growling or snapping, that dogs are directing towards others. We know the behaviour might have arisen because the dog keeps encountering the trigger and feeling they need to actively avoid it or escape. So, if we can create scenarios where they encounter the trigger but find they do not need to take action, we can start to tip the balance away from those proactive distance-increasing behaviours. Exposure should be low intensity: this can be achieved by using greater distances between dog and trigger, and/or picking triggers that move less, make less noise, or are very predictable. Once the dog can notice the trigger and come to accept that they don't need to act on it, they start to relax; this is a form of desensitisation. Desensitisation is a proven method for treating many problem behaviours that have emotional drivers.

In defence of small dogs

Small dogs are often labelled as being overly bossy or having 'Napoleon syndrome' or 'small dog syndrome' because of their tendency to readily employ distance-increasing behaviours. These can include barking, lunging, rushing, growling and snapping, as well as escape and avoidance (e.g. running away). Small dogs live in a world of giants. They are comparatively fragile, and even a friendly giant can hurt them if the play is too rough. Conversely, a small dog's capacity to stand up for herself is limited by how far she can escalate matters. Kestrel, at 5.2 kg (11 lb) will certainly stand up for herself, but if a 30 kg (5 stone) Labrador retriever like Bundy is galumphing over the top of her she may as well be a grasshopper standing up to an elephant. Even when small dogs are trying to move away, some large dogs (and many humans) approach to greet them. It is little wonder that many small dogs learn to switch to a more forceful strategy. When all the whispers, polite requests and active attempts to avoid fail, but yelling

Crouching and allowing the dog to come to you makes you seem much less threatening.

sometimes works, then yelling will become the preferred option. Small dogs cannot be judged poorly for making that choice: life is not so easy for them. Next time you encounter a small dog, take the time to think what might have influenced their behaviour. Help them out by giving them the opportunity to be master of their own destiny and have a choice in how the interaction proceeds.

Fear is the sum of its parts

Fear of unpleasant or undesired outcomes can be a fundamental predictor of how a dog behaves. Some negative outcomes, such as pain, are intimately associated with fear, whereas others are less certain. Dogs can learn to fear their space being invaded, but often this can be broken down further into what they dread so much about this invasion. Is it fear of uncertainty, loss of control, or is it as simple as a fear that the encounter will become aggressive or boisterous, which can lead to pain? We've already discussed what dogs sense, so we might run through possible noxious stimuli. Is there a loud or strange sound? Is there unusual pressure on some part of the dog's body? Is there some rapid or unpredictable movement? We can build on this by considering what might be unusual, confusing, or threatening stimuli to the dog. We can guess at what our dogs fear by observing what they attempt to escape from, but this is likely a clumsy interpretation of our dogs' emotional states. Just like humans, dogs can experience anxiety about what might happen as well as fear of what is happening, and that may be more difficult to detect.

Small dogs are inherently vulnerable. It is easy for them to learn to become very defensive.

4

HOW DO YOU KNOW IF YOUR DOG IS HAPPY?

WHAT DO WE REALLY WANT FROM OUR RELATIONSHIPS WITH OUR DOGS?

Since you are reading a book about making dogs happy it seems safe to assume that you: a) believe dogs can be happy; b) want the dogs in your care to be happy; and c) believe we can tell if dogs are happy. You probably don't need to hear a careful, evidence-based argument for why we want happy dogs. However, answering these questions is a useful process in understanding what we want from the relationship — and it also provides a handy comeback if someone sniggers at you for fretting about your dog's emotional state and life happiness. Dog happiness is a serious business. Sniggering will be met with a brutal, scientifically credible putdown.

Can dogs be 'happy'?

Firstly, it is generally frowned upon in scientific circles to say any animal is 'happy'. This isn't because scientists don't believe animals have emotions, particularly such basic emotions as 'happiness', but because the word describes an emotional state that humans understand. The concept of happiness is cultural for humans, and we are not sure if an animal experiences what we would call 'happiness' in the same way that we do. However, we do know that dogs and other mammals seek out certain stimuli. We know that when non-human animals access these stimuli, their neural activities are similar to ours

Studies show dogs see their owner's approach as a big reward.
(They may not even wait for the owner to finish approaching.)

when we are in a positive emotional state. We know that when animals have enriched lives and access to items or activities they value, they tend to expect more positive outcomes for themselves than negative outcomes. This optimism is not exactly 'happiness', but is considered indicative of a positive emotional state. Regardless of whether that be described as happiness, joy, contentment, bliss, or something we humans have never quite experienced, we can be confident it's good.

We also know that a dog has a reward centre in its brain and has the same neurotransmitters, which go to roughly the same places in the dog brain as they do in the human brain when we feel rewarded. We know that we like being rewarded and it often makes us feel happy. We know that the parts of the brain that are active during rewarding episodes for dogs are also active when dogs see and hear their owners. This effect is specific to their owners, not just to people in general, so we can infer that dogs find us to be rewarding company.

So, strictly speaking, although we are not sure if dogs can be happy, we are very confident they can experience positive emotional states, both short-term and long-term, which are at least similar to what we humans feel as 'happiness'.

Why should we want our dogs to be happy?

Most humans are empathetic and compassionate creatures. We want those we love to be happy. We particularly want those we nurture and care for to be happy. Maybe it reflects well on us socially when we are successful nurturers? Perhaps we also feel an urge to reciprocate dogs for the joy they give us. Perhaps we recognise and feel the need to compensate for the lack of agency and autonomy that so often comes with being our companions, as they depend on us for food, water and exercise. Given that they make us so happy (usually), it's only fair that we try to make them happy in turn. Beyond simple reciprocation, there are also practical reasons why we might want happy dogs, and these hark back to emotional states and optimism again. Dogs who experience positive emotional states often tend to be more optimistic. This can mean they are more willing to try new behaviours, and are more resilient when life does not go their way. Their human caretakers can find them very easy to train and they may recover easily when something unexpected, or even unpleasant, happens. Such resilience is particularly highly sought in working roles that require great persistence and sometimes involve discomfort or even pain, such as scent detection dogs and police, military or security dogs. These dogs must comprehend that humans might try to hurt them. For our companion dogs, resilience can provide an effective buffer against unexpected negative outcomes. Anyone with a pessimistic dog that lacks resilience probably has an idea of the sheer number of events that might have unexpected negative outcomes for their dog. Everyday sounds, such as a tin can being closed, everyday interventions like a harness going on over the head, and apparently innocuous appearances, such as a ball bouncing past unexpectedly, can all be enough to create aversion to those events and the stimuli related to them. The dog afraid of a tin can might avoid the kitchen in general. The emergence of the harness could vanquish the positive associations with exercise. The bouncing ball at the wrong moment could result in the dog avoiding a particular behaviour, place or person.

Not only do such aversions compromise a dog's wellbeing, but they can also make life difficult for owners. For example, with the accumulation of aversions in the form of car-sickness, fear of strangers and phobia of the clinic, some owners need to sedate their dogs for vet visits. This is far from ideal and a sedated patient is difficult to assess fully during the veterinary examination.

How can we tell if a dog is happy?

This is the million dollar question. Obviously, dogs can't speak our language, so they can't tell us directly how they are feeling. Instead, we are limited to inferring a dog's emotional state using non-invasive indicators. Happy dogs show signs of their state in two detectable ways: 1) through their body language; and 2) through the decisions they make and the activities they engage in.

For the purposes of this discussion, emotional states are not specific emotions such as jealousy, anger, joy and so on. As discussed, it might not be appropriate to use these labels for the emotions that non-human animals experience. Rather, we are identifying broad emotional states that can be thought of as containing two components. The first is 'emotional valence', which captures a sense of how positive or negative the experience is. It is fair to assume this exists on a continuum for dogs and other animals, with positive at one end and negative at the other. The second component is 'arousal', which refers to how strong the experience is. High arousal is associated with a higher heart rate, sweating (dogs sweat only from their paws), panting, physical activity, increased muscle tension and narrowing of focus. Low arousal is associated with calmness, slow movement and relaxed muscles. It is critical to appreciate both the arousal and valence components — dogs tend to behave dramatically differently if just one component changes. A dog experiencing positive valence and high arousal might race around in play, while a dog experiencing positive valence and low arousal could be lying down and playing a gentle game of mouthing a toy. A dog experiencing negative valence and high arousal might be in a state of panic with fight, flight or freeze seeming the only options, while a dog experiencing negative valence and low arousal might quietly move away from the cause of the negative valence. So, spotting a happy dog requires us to look for evidence of positive valence at all levels of arousal. This is trickier than it sounds, but let's begin with the more obvious manifestations of positive valence.

Everyone with a dog is probably (hopefully!) familiar with the unbridled enthusiasm of an apparently joyful dog cavorting around, expending energy like a pre-schooler with a secret red cordial stash. Energy is a finite resource for animals, and spending it on activities that are not important for survival or reproduction suggests the activity has a different purpose. But cavorting is the high-arousal expression of happiness. How can we tell if a dog is enjoying a sedate walk along the beach? How do we tell the difference between a contented dog resting and one that is inactive due to a state of depression? Dog body language can assist, if we know what to look for. It is a general rule that 'loose' dogs are comfortable dogs. Next time your dog is having a good sniff around in the bushes, look at what her body is doing and how freely she moves.

Telling tails

If your dog has a tail, she might give you a sense of how much oomph she is using it with. Is she wagging it in flexible sweeps, which perhaps wrap around mugs on coffee tables and fling them across the room? Or is physical contact with the wagging tail more like having a ruler slapped against your shins? Depending on the breed, the tail could be held high, straight or low, and might be wagging fast, slow or not at all, but the telling characteristic is how relaxed the whole tail is.

The speed and height of the tail wag contain information about the arousal and alertness of the dog. High tails are usually associated with keen alertness and perhaps signal a willingness to take a forward approach to a given situation. This can be hard to detect in breeds with a naturally high tail carriage, such as spitz breeds, or those with lower tail carriages, such as German shepherd dogs.

Loose tail wags indicate positive states. High, stiff tails indicate arousal, which can be either positive or negative.

When two dogs meet and both have high tails, we ought to watch closely and err on the side of caution by calling one or both away after a few seconds if at least one doesn't show some tail-lowering and/or relaxation in the rest of their body in order to avoid an escalation in arousal and subsequent increased likelihood of aggression. In contrast, a low tail tends to signify the dog's willingness to let someone else take charge of the situation. Dogs greeting humans often wag their tails fast and low — to signal they are mere dogs in the presence of greatness.

It is also good to check out joints such as hips, knees, shoulders and elbows. If there is enough room for the dog to show unfettered movement, an absence of tension manifests in a dog that takes easy, fully extended strides. However, it is important to note that high arousal in a situation that calls for restraint can produce clipped, mincing steps as the dog tries to keep a lid on their excitement, so they won't leap on you and provoke a negative consequence, such as being shouted at or shoved away.

Other signs of happiness

Your dog's face and ears can be very communicative. Look at the corners of your dog's mouth, the muscles around his eyes and the way the ears are carried. Relaxed mouths and eyes move more than tight mouths and eyes. The mouth is likely to change shape more often than in a tense dog, and the commissures (corners) of the mouth might droop downwards. (Note: This is not a helpful cue if you own a bulldog! The faces of bulldogs, Boxers, and other breeds with loose flews or wrinkles can be particularly difficult to read. You need to look closely at the spaces between wrinkles or changes in how the wrinkles sit.) Ears of dogs who are awake, but relaxed, sit at roughly 10 and 2 o'clock around the dog's face and point forwards and slightly out to the side; obviously with some breed differences.

Dogs with ears that droop do show this, but it's only visible where the ears join the head. As dogs become more intensely interested in a stimulus, their arousal climbs, and their ears will lift higher on their heads until they face straight ahead. When ears are at their highest, often some wrinkles will form between them on the dog's forehead. In contrast, when signalling adoration, dogs tend to move their ears so that they hang down and back with the tips lying facing down alongside the dog's neck. This is how dogs tell you they are gazing upon a demi-god human genius.

It's not so hard to tell if a dog enjoys an activity when he is moderately to highly aroused. Aroused dogs express their joy in expending energy, but seasoned dog-watchers also notice a certain looseness throughout the dog's body, known as low postural tonus. This refers to a lack of tension in the skeletal muscles that dogs use to support their posture. High postural tonus is seen in tension through the body, but does not necessarily mean the dog is unhappy. Dogs can be tense and focused and still enjoy what they are doing.

A dog who is ready to chase a ball can be the epitome of fierce concentration while devoid of motion. So how do we know if a dog likes chasing balls? Well, a great litmus test is to fall back on operant conditioning to see if throwing a ball can be used to reinforce behaviour. For example, if you ask your dog to sit and then throw the ball for her when she does so, you just need to work out whether she sits quicker, or more often, or for longer, when you have the ball in your hand? Or the evidence might be even more obvious than that. If your dog keeps bringing that ball back to you and each time you throw it again, then we can assume bringing the ball back is reinforced by getting to chase the ball again. What about the dog that chases the ball every time, but doesn't bring it back? The key here is to realise that for chasing the ball to continue, the dog might not actually need to bring it back; for example, if you go over and get the ball. And some dogs are so eager to possess the ball that they can't seem to decide if they want to give it to you to throw again or just hold onto it. Their internal conflict is between chase and possession. Either way, we can be sure that the ball is highly valued.

How can we tell if a dog is unhappy?

We covered in Chapter 3 the stimuli, sensations, events and conditions that dogs generally do not like. But, there are endless objects in the world that a dog might find concerning, threatening, distressing or downright terrifying. Dogs that are experiencing extreme distress are easy to identify. They will flee the area, hide, tremble, drool, pant heavily, their tail is held down and tight against their belly and they will often adopt a hunched posture with their body lowered, as if they are desperately clinging to the ground for fear the world is about to be turned upside-down. Their ears are held flat against their head and turned outwards, or folded partially back and facing outwards. And their eyes often show more white (the technical term is sclera), creating a so-called 'whale eye'.

More subtle signs of distress and fear are not difficult to see if one knows what to look for. Just as the hallmark of a happy dog is a loose body, the hallmark of a distressed dog is a tense body. Tension can be seen in the way a dog moves with clipped steps and limited flexion in the knees or elbows.

If the dog is still, you can still see tension, but you might need to look closely. Tension around a dog's mouth is best detected at the corners and looks like a tight smile — the kind you might shoot at someone who just said your interior decorating is 'busy'. Your tight smile won't

The puppy has his ears back, suggesting worry, but his body and face are relaxed. Call the older dog away for a break.

reach your eyes, which will instead remain still and somewhat glassy. Likewise, tension around a dog's eyes is best detected through their lack of movement. Sometimes it's possible to see a small bulge underneath the lower eyelid and towards the outer corners of the eyes where the orbicularis oculi muscle (used to close the eyelids) can become bunched-up. Sometimes it is also possible to see a little squint, where the corners of the eyes are tight. However, don't mistake this for a submissive squint, where the eyelids are partially closed to create the appearance of narrow eyes. Dogs that are trying to tell you they want no trouble can also squint, but that is usually a soft close of the eyelids rather than tight corners, and usually accompanied by a closed mouth.

Just walk on by

Dogs will often try to avoid stimuli that are threatening to them, but this is not always obvious. They use the direction of their gaze to signal to other social partners (dogs, humans and possibly other pets) whether they are interested in interacting or not. A dog that has politely looked away from another dog and at a spot on the ground somewhere beside or slightly in front of it is attempting to communicate 'Thanks, but no thanks' to the other dog. (Kind of like when you're in the supermarket and you see someone you knew in high school but you don't feel like talking to them, so you stare into the distance and pretend you haven't seen them.)

This subtle signal is often missed by other dogs themselves, so it is a great one for owners to be aware of. If you see your dog doing this, it is a good cue to call them and move them away from the other dog (or child, or adult). This will help ensure their polite strategies are effective.

For some dogs, after they say 'Thanks, but no thanks' and the other dog doesn't move away, the next thing they say, particularly if several 'no thanks' have been ignored, is: 'THAT'S IT! SO HELP ME, I WILL BITE YOU!' Some dogs have limited patience, just like some humans do. However, for most dogs, the next attempt at communication is actively moving away, if physical avoidance is an option. This is not running away. It is casual walking away, at a tangent. A lowered head and tail will generally signal the dog's disinterest in continuing the interaction. When a dog walks away, please let them go. They are often trying to leave a situation they are not comfortable with. If they can't leave quietly, they will have to resort to other strategies to increase the distance between them and the source of unpleasantness, and this is when we see snarls, growling, hackles raised, ears either forward and up in threat or flat against the head in fear, and barks and snaps. These behaviours are signals that the dog can't move away itself and so is strongly recommending that the source of its displeasure moves away instead.

We humans often seem outraged that our canine pal could behave like this. Does he not understand that he is supposed to be friendly? It is definitely not cool to threaten others! He doesn't know this, though, and even if he did, he wouldn't care. Imagine you are in a crowded bus and someone is standing almost on top of you. You carefully avoid eye contact. They lean towards you, and you're not sure what their intentions are, so you lean away from them and glare. Dogs behave similarly when they encounter in-your-face proximity. They glare too, as it happens. They become very still, lower their heads and stare right in the eyes of their new adversary with their ears pricked up and forward. As with humans, a dog glare means negative consequences are imminent. The crowded bus menace doesn't seem to notice your glare though and, however inadvertently, touches your hair with his hand. You swipe the hand away, just as a dog would growl. But the hand drifts back towards you almost immediately. Your heart is

pounding. You do not feel safe. What is this person going to do next? You don't want to escalate the situation still further, but what options do you have? It's a crowded bus: you can't move away. They lean over again. You don't know what they are going to do, but you're not about to wait passively to find out. Instead you burst into a loud yell, physically fend them off and yell a bit more for good measure. The person sitting next to you on the bus scolds you for being rude: 'He was only being friendly!' But, you know the intruder was the one being rude and you behaved the way you felt you had to.

The dog world is much the same. What is friendly to one dog is extraordinarily rude to another, and offended dogs have every right to express their dissent. However, that doesn't mean we have to leave them in situations where they need to express their discomfort. Imagine if you were on that bus glaring at the rude passenger and a friend of yours suddenly appeared and suggested you both move to the back of the bus. That's a good friend! Be your dog's friend and bail him out when he is having an unpleasant social interaction.

Problems, problems, problems — when conflicting goals compete

Let's return to the dog who won't give her ball back to you. She chases the ball with abandon when you throw it, and cavorts around with it when she captures it but, while she will bring it most of the way back to you and put it on the ground, she keeps trying to grab it every time you reach for it.

What's going on? Does she like chasing the ball or not? If she is displaying her happy body language when waiting for you to throw the ball and/or when chasing it and possessing it, then we can assume

The Dalmatian is showing his teeth to buy space. The other dog gets the message loud and clear, indicating 'peace'.

she probably likes that part at least. But, she is a dog, and dogs have evolved to be selfish opportunists. Her brain is hard-wired to incline her to take what she wants and try to keep it for as long as possible. She loves playing with the ball, and probably wants the play to continue, but relinquishing an item she values is to her a woeful strategy for retaining resources. She has competing goals: play ball, and keep the ball. This can result in a tortured game of chasing the ball, bringing it back, dropping it, grabbing it when anyone tries to reach for it, dropping it again, grabbing it again, dropping it again, bouncing impatiently, grabbing it, dropping it, barking, grabbing it and so on. In another manifestation of this conflict, she might not bring it back, but instead carry it around with her, watching you all the time. She might bring it towards you, but, as if by accident, drop it several metres away from you. She might let you pick it up and then abruptly try to snatch it from you again. This kind of internal conflict can arise in all kinds of situations and some dogs might show it more obviously than others.

Neville nominates the best stick to carry on each and every walk and he plays with it ostentatiously when Bundy is watching. He often drops it as if he has lost interest and wanders off but woe betide Bundy if he dares to pick up the stick *du jour*. Neville races back to dispossess Bundy: the value of the stick has been confirmed.

Dogs express their conflict in different ways — some more obviously by far than others. While Kestrel produces a range of fascinating vocalisations when she is beset with competing goals, Kivi merely tilts his ears outwards and backwards just a little, and maybe licks his lips. There is no evidence that a response like Kestrel's indicates stronger emotion than Kivi's response. Indeed, some research suggests that the quiet sufferer might even have a more negative experience than the more expressive individual. Other expressive signs of conflict may include physical movement, such as shuffling or jumping, and some dogs are extremely expressive, defaulting to rushing forwards while barking. Other more passive ways of expressing conflict include holding up a front paw, glancing in different directions, looking away, yawning or sniffing the ground. It's important to appreciate that many of these behaviours can also occur in contexts when a dog is not conflicted, so, on their own, they are not reliable signs. If the dog is also hesitating, moving closer and then further away from an object, whining, or dancing around as if he can't make up his mind where to go, these are good indicators that the dog is in a state of conflict.

Help ease your dog's self-conflict

Is conflict bad? It is probably relative to how much conflict is being experienced and whether the dog can resolve it easily. Generally, it is unpleasant for us humans to feel indecisive or pulled in two different directions by competing goals, but there are degrees of unpleasantness. A conflict may barely register for that moment we couldn't decide whether to cross the road now and walk in the shade or cross the road at the next corner and go past that shop we like first, but the internal conflict around whether or not we should confront a stranger who is behaving poorly in public can raise our heart rate, make us sweat and even feel ill.

The conflict in a dog who wants to both possess the ball and relinquish it to play fetch might be considerable, as these goals are thoroughly incompatible and the dog could very much want to obtain both. The conflict in a dog who wants to both run around the house excitedly and also get her leash on so she can go for a walk might be less intense. A dog can find a sweet spot that satisfies both goals to some extent by dancing and barking while she gets her leash on. If we refuse to put on her leash until she sits calmly, we ratchet up that sense of conflict because we are reducing her ability to satisfy both goals. However, we can help her resolve this conflict; for example, if we offer her an extra reinforcer, such as a treat if she can sit calmly to have her leash on, we have now added another excellent reason for her to choose sitting calmly over wriggling, which reduces the conflict we heightened by expecting calm behaviour.

Another possibility is asking the dog for only a moment of calm behaviour and reinforcing that response by putting the leash on. This way, the conflict is only momentary rather than prolonged, so it is less intense. Asking for calm behaviour for just a little longer on each successive occasion builds the dog's tolerance of that conflict as she practises the self-control required to behave calmly while she would also like to be running around excitedly.

Ease a dog's conflict about putting the leash on by using food to help them remain calm and hold still.

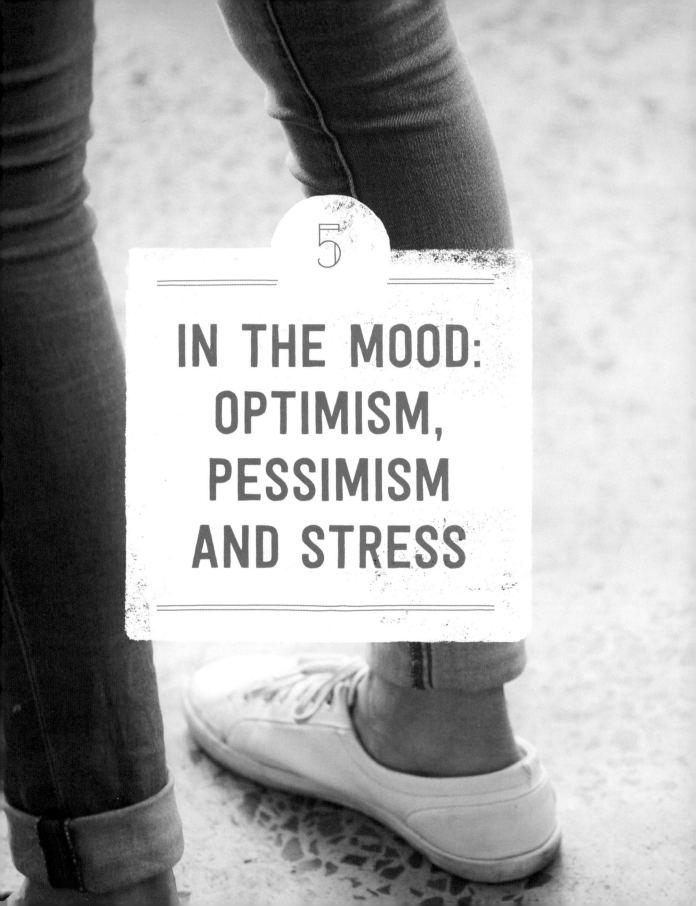

5

IN THE MOOD: OPTIMISM, PESSIMISM AND STRESS

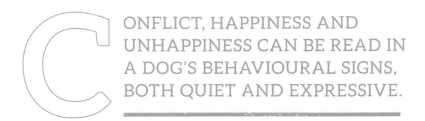

CONFLICT, HAPPINESS AND UNHAPPINESS CAN BE READ IN A DOG'S BEHAVIOURAL SIGNS, BOTH QUIET AND EXPRESSIVE.

It is essential that we read these transient states, because all moment-to-moment emotional experiences contribute to dogs' long-term emotional states and influence how they perceive their world.

It has been said that dogs live in the present, rather than dwelling on the past or worrying about the future. While that may be debatable, it doesn't rule out the prospect that dogs can have long-term emotional states, or what we generally refer to as 'moods'. Mood is heavily influenced by the perception of risk. In turn, how risky a situation feels to a dog has a strong effect on the behaviours they might display. These behaviours then have a strong effect on how the situation plays out and whether the dog gets closer to his goals, and the intensity of the emotional experience associated with that situation. Always, there is a balance between taking risks and avoiding possible danger.

The saying 'nothing ventured, nothing gained' is as pertinent to dogs as it is to humans. Risk-averse dogs generally do not venture and consequently fail to gain. As they avoid risks, the world remains known and thus safe to them, but new experiences that could be rewarding are out of their reach.

Optimistic dogs, who are willing to risk negative or even largely neutral outcomes, discover reinforcers everywhere they go. Dogs adjust their outlook on life according to their accumulation of

Lip licking in dogs can indicate conflict or discomfort.

experiences. We can imagine that a dog who remains in a small but safe world, avoiding risk, might have a much smaller accumulation of good experiences than a relatively bold dog, who is forever finding new sources of reinforcers. Recent experiences may play a larger role than distant ones, but intense experiences are well remembered, regardless of how long ago they occurred. This makes sense, because it pays to remember both excellent and terrible outcomes to navigate towards or around them in future. We should be able to relate to this; after all, humans recall their most emotional memories most vividly.

TURNING THE TABLES ON RISK-TAKING

Kivi is not a risk-taker by nature, and his first few years did not encourage him to become one. If, as a pup, he had a problem, he would whine until his humans solved it for him. It was discovered that this reliance on humans and their willingness to assist had resulted in his dismal problem-solving skills. Stepping over a branch on a trail would leave him crying piteously on the other side, helpless to join the group and greatly distressed. Being a PhD student studying optimism in dogs, Melissa endeavoured to fix this. Kivi was rewarded for jumping onto and over obstacles, and was encouraged to find his own way through tiny problems such as his humans being on the wrong side of a small creek. He successfully learned to find alternative routes and proactively solve his problems by taking risks, instead of defaulting to crying. More than simply sparing him the distress of being unable to instantly and easily reach his goals, this approach opened an entire world he had never known before. He started seeking obstacles to tackle and this brought him to discover many exciting smells and animal carcasses in varying states of decomposition suitable for eating and rolling in. Dogs find interest in their world wherever they go, but only if they are bold enough to investigate. Some dogs are not inherently optimistic enough to embrace that boldness on their own, but can be encouraged to take risks. It is most important that these be small risks that are sure to pay off. Bundy has a dislike for shiny floors and must be given plenty of time and quiet encouragement when he engages with them. This helps him remain calm and thus avoids him picking up speed, which can lead to slipping, which in turn makes his paws clench and leads to a loss of traction and resultant panic.

Dogmanship acknowledges the need to read dogs and respond accordingly. Dogs can't explain their moods to us, but it's possible to make an educated guess by looking at their behaviour and how they seem to interpret the world around them.

Did someone just drop a sausage in the next suburb?

Attentiveness to potentially rewarding signals is a good indication that your dog might be feeling optimistic. The sound of an object hitting the floor warrants instant investigation for the dog that expects positive outcomes. The object could be edible! Erik thinks a wordless exclamation is an excellent reason to run into the room and check the floor. However, we should be cautious in our interpretation of this: Erik is fast, and clumsy Melissa often drops edible items on the floor, so it's likely his learning history could trigger decisions and behaviours that look the same as long-term optimism but cannot be confirmed as such. It would be more enlightening to consider broad patterns of responses. Does the dog generally check out any signal that potentially relates to food availability? Even more enlightening would be to look at how a dog's decisions correspond to his prior experiences. A signal that often heralds a positive outcome (e.g. a wordless exclamation in the kitchen) can be responded to without much optimism; whereas a signal only occasionally associated with a positive outcome (e.g. a wordless exclamation in the backyard) requires more optimism to respond to. Also, the energy cost of checking an uncertain outcome is revealing. A dog who gets up from another room to journey outside and check on that wordless exclamation is probably feeling lucky.

Tracking optimism and how prior experiences influence it can give us a good idea of how positive our dogs are feeling on an ongoing basis. Monitoring a dog's participation in activities that he is known to enjoy (we discussed these signs of enjoyment in Chapter 4) might alert you to declines in positive mood. A sudden change in his enjoyment or the frequency with which he participates in an activity that he has historically enjoyed is certainly cause for investigation. That is why *doglogbook* was developed: as a means to monitor the joy dogs take in life and the way these trend over time.

SURPRISE ME!

Changes in optimism/pessimism in response to changes in the environment tend to be transient. So, for example, dogs might at first respond very positively to an extra walk each day, but over a few weeks they adapt to the new routine and their optimism returns to its level before the extra walk was added. This tells us that we don't need to be too obsessed with filling our dogs' lives with positive outcomes and environmental enrichment, but can instead provide positive 'surprises' every week or so to boost positive mood on a regular basis. It's easy to surprise most dogs: a toy they haven't seen in a while, a walk in a different area or an unexpected food will likely do it. Many dogs seem even more delighted if they happen to discover surprises for themselves. It's fun to leave them presents where they will find them during their exploratory activities, either at home or out and about.

Long-term moods

It is harder to assess long-term positive moods in our dogs. A dog's enjoyment of some activities can naturally decline as he ages and he might also refine his activities so that he does less of them, but the quality of engagement increases. Casual monitoring of his participation in activities over time is therefore not necessarily revealing of his long-term mood. Even a gradual decline in enthusiasm for walks or chew treats such as bones warrants checking, and this can be done by collecting information with tools such as *doglogbook*. Detecting such patterns enables dog owners to adjust their behaviour to support their dog as he matures. (Still, whenever you spot such a trend, it is worth a veterinary check to ensure there is no pain that might account for his change in behaviour.) When does the dog still participate in the particular activity? Are there times he no longer participates? Are there places where he will participate and others where he won't? Are there individuals with whom he will interact and others with whom he won't? Investigating the variability in his participation is a good way to expose patterns. Maybe he participates in quiet parks but no longer in busy parks? This suggests it might be the environment that is the problem. Maybe he participates with small dogs but no longer with large dogs, which suggests his participation is dependent on the company.

Melissa's older dogs will play on occasion with strange dogs but, after years learning each other's play styles, most of their play has become

The Labrador is clearly uncomfortable with the other dog being so close. The tension in her face shows her unhappiness.

with each other. They know each other well, so are responsive to each other's signals, there is very little chance of making a mistake, and their relationship is firm enough that forgiveness is easy anyway. They can relax in their play and be less constrained than is needed with dogs they don't know so well. This contrasts with when they were young and would play with any dog who appeared willing.

As dog watchers and *dogloggers*, we can also collect information about how much opportunity our dogs have to participate in activities we know they enjoy. Did we used to take them out twice a day, but now only do so once a day? The change might have been for a good reason, or it might have been a temporary change that became permanent. The dog might show no change in her behaviour, but how would she express missing that extra walk? How would her behaviour express her appreciation of an extra walk if we added one? We might see changes in her activity level at home that correspond to more walks or fewer walks. We might find she takes herself to bed with a chew item more readily when she has had more walks, or equally, she may chew more when she has had fewer walks if she is frustrated with the decreased activity. She may bark less, or spend less time trying to solicit play from disinterested humans or dogs when she has had more outings. She might be less aroused when out walking and more responsive as a result. All these small changes hint at the extra walk having a positive influence on her mood, but we would never know if we didn't try it more than once and monitor how she responded in the medium term each time.

When life takes a turn for the worse

A risk-averse dog is not necessarily an unhappy dog. Personality plays a role in how individuals perceive the world, and dogs can be risk-averse and still find plenty of joy in their life. It might be possible to help risk-averse dogs learn to try new behaviours or activities and thus access more reinforcers in their daily life, but there are situations where this risk-aversion or specific negative expectations can dominate their lives.

Consider Dog A is visiting the park and Dog B approaches him. Whether, because he is already in a negative state or because he has learned to expect poor outcomes with strange dogs, A views B and has the expectation that any interaction with B will turn out poorly for him. At this point, A probably wants B to go away so he doesn't have to handle the possible negative outcome, but B doesn't go. Dog B might try to make the best of the situation and start with a relatively typical canine greeting — it doesn't matter if that goes well or poorly, because A is looking for signals that it's going to turn sour, so that he can try to stay safe. Dog B bounces a little, and that looks threatening to A purely because he is already expecting a negative outcome. So, A suddenly lunges at B with a growl to demand more space so he can feel safer. Dog B responds by lunging back and barking. The owners of both dogs drag them apart. Dog B has learned that some dogs are unpredictable and not much fun. Dog A has learned that he was right to expect a negative outcome; he does not appreciate that he was the one who caused it. The next time A sees a strange dog, his prior experiences tell him he is even more likely to have a negative outcome. He reacts accordingly with more caution, and is ready to use his distance-increasing behaviours, such as growling and lunging, at the slightest hint he might need more distance to be safe, and so he creates another negative outcome. With each such experience, Dog A's negative expectations intensify, even though he might be creating many of the negative experiences himself. Being dragged away from other dogs by his owner makes matters worse, because the sight of other dogs predicts discomfort or even pain around his neck.

It is possible for this self-perpetuating pessimism to become globalised, and a dog to experience similar pessimism regarding other stimuli, such as loud noises, human visitors, cars, trades people, etc. If a dog has negative outcomes often enough, he will start to anticipate them in more contexts. A resultant state of anxiety might influence expectations and can also influence how every event is interpreted as it occurs, creating an inescapable spiral of depression. (We don't know exactly if dogs can be depressed in the same way as humans, but there is evidence to suggest animals might experience emotional states that are at least similar to depression. This is usually referred to as anhedonia, which means an inability to experience pleasure.) The dog's negative expectations have become so strong and pervasive that his subsequent risk aversion prevents him from locating reinforcers. What little joy he did have also starts to diminish. This may be the case for many dogs who end up in shelters: they have lost track of how to have fun and need to be understood as such.

Successful and unsuccessful coping

Stress visits every animal on a regular basis; that is part of life. All species are exquisitely well adapted to coping with stimuli and events that cause stress (stressors). We know that stress in many forms can be psychologically damaging and, when chronic, is known to be associated with physical and mental illnesses in humans. In dogs, it might also be associated with reduced lifespan and health issues such as skin disorders. It has been argued that the impact of stress on an individual boils down to how successfully he or she copes with it. The concept of successful coping is not easy to pin down, even in humans. For example, is successful coping eliminating stress entirely, or is it

Too many negative experiences and
encounters can make a dog pessimistic.

simply a matter of minimising psychological distress? Does the cost of eliminating or minimising the stress matter?

Imagine Dog C dislikes other dogs. While out walking with his human one day, C sees Dog D and tries to charge over and bark furiously at him. This is a distance-increasing behaviour — C is trying to compel D to move away. Dog C is on a leash, though, so he can't reach D, but C still performs the same behaviour sequence repeatedly. Why does he keep doing it when it doesn't seem to achieve anything? The answer is that it probably does move him closer towards his goals. It's likely that other dogs are going to be moved away by their owners while C is barking and lunging: this gets him closer to his goal of creating more distance between himself and the other dogs, so that alone might be enough for him to persist with this behaviour. However, expending all that energy may also help to both alleviate the heightened arousal he experiences when he first sees another dog, and make him feel he has some control over the situation. Both of those outcomes could be relatively positive for him. It is a semi-successful coping strategy in that the stressors (the other dogs) go away, sooner or later. But, C expends an awful lot of energy achieving this, and the high arousal state he gets into when he sees another dog is all about preparing him to act to meet potential threats.

What is the psychological impact of being highly aroused due to the proximity of potential threats? It is most likely unpleasant. Indeed, some dogs get so aroused and frustrated that they will even turn around and bite their owner or another dog they live with. Doing so may alleviate some of the tension and anxiety that come from being in such a highly aroused state, but it undoubtedly damages their social relationships. As such, it is a coping strategy that might be successful

The Dalmatian is leaning away from these intense dogs and would like more space.

in approaching one goal (alleviating tension), but at the cost of a second goal (positive relationships with social group members). What if we showed C that if he stays with his owner, he gets treats, and that D and all of the other dogs still go away, or their owners move them away before he even has to start barking and lunging? This simple and humane coping strategy is effective, and is also efficient, and comes without the unpleasant, highly aroused state. It connects C with his owner rather than risking their relationship. So, for our purposes as dog owners who want happy dogs, let's assume that 'successful coping' means effective, and does not have a negative effect on other primary goals such as social harmony or access to valued resources.

A dog failing to cope successfully with stress is likely to show one or more of a variety of behavioural symptoms. Just as humans can adopt coping strategies that do them more harm than good, so can dogs. Dogs might become hypervigilant, scanning their environment for potential dangers even when there is unlikely to be any. They might become volatile — over-reacting to relatively benign stimuli that they used to take in their stride. They may find it difficult to sleep because they need to be attentive to small signs of potential threat. They could be restless — just like humans in a hospital waiting room who are often too anxious to sit and relax. They might go off their food, drink more water, become destructive, start urinating or defecating indoors, become less tolerant of their human and canine friends, or lose interest in playing. Some could discover self-soothing behaviours to help them cope, such as sucking on or licking objects or themselves, or engaging in other compulsive activities such as pacing or chasing shadows/flies/light reflections/their tail. These activities may be difficult to interrupt or dogs might become distressed if they can't perform them. They might also start to guard areas of security from other animals or humans (even their owners). This is the picture of a dog who is chronically stressed and failing to cope successfully with the situation. Failing to cope successfully with stress is an awful experience for humans; and one that often requires professional help. It is the same for dogs. A veterinarian with an interest in animal behaviour can often provide that professional help. An animal behaviourist might be able to assist, but interventions are most successful when training is combined with clinical help.

Ensuring your dog copes successfully

We can apply this successful coping idea to other scenarios. Can a dog going to the veterinarian willingly enter the examination room? If she won't, there is already going to be a problem, because she will be, however gently, forced in and then her coping strategies will be limited to buying space aggressively, escaping by fleeing, or enduring. Fighting and fleeing are both unlikely to result in the stressor going away — at least not permanently — so are likely to result in unsuccessful coping (and potentially serious danger to herself, her owner and her veterinarian). If she opts for enduring, she may habituate to the challenge, which means she gets used to the situation and thus it becomes less distressing. If she does not habituate, then she cannot cope successfully. You can see that her chances of learning to successfully cope with visits to the veterinarian are low.

What about Dog E, who will go into the examination room willingly, but resists having his teeth checked? He is also forced into cooperation and the strategies he adopts to cope with the examination depend on how unpleasant it is for him. If it is mildly unpleasant, E might try to move away from the vet, or give some of his signals for 'Thanks, but no thanks' (see page 100). We know that if the unpleasant stimulus does not go away, he could escalate his requests for space to overt aggression. If the examination ends there, E might learn that aggression is an effective strategy. If it does not, he could escalate again, or he might switch to a different strategy of tolerance until such time as he can escape. None of these options is good for any dog's mental wellbeing. Being robbed of control, as discussed in Chapter 3, is a major problem for dogs. They are handled in ways that don't make sense to them and that they might find painful and/or threatening. And on top of that, the few coping strategies that are available to them read like a catalogue of dog behaviour problems.

This is a great argument for taking the time to gain your dog's willing cooperation in their own husbandry. Dogs will accept a lot of uncomfortable sensations if they are paid handsomely for doing so, and the super-dedicated dog owner will give their dog a choice to leave at any time, and try again in a short while if the dog is prepared to cooperate. A combination of trust that they can choose not to participate and won't be forced, coupled with reinforcement when they do choose to participate, can result in dogs who have positive experiences during grooming and veterinary checks, and have ways to tell their owner when they are no longer comfortable.

This keeps their stress to a minimum, fosters a brilliant bond based on trust with their owners and gives them successful, calm, acceptable coping strategies.

Does successful coping always mean positive welfare?

Here is a different scenario. Dog F in the dog park is visited by Dog G, who is invading her space. Dog F uses her 'Thanks, but no thanks' signals and G blessedly turns aside and walks away. Dog F has disengaged from an uncomfortable situation with a strange dog without using excessive energy and with minimal risk to herself and

Your hand has an invisible string between it and your dog's nose. Use it to lure your dog into position.

her other social relationships. This meets our definition for successful coping. Did F like the interaction? It is fair to say she did not want it to continue. She might have simply had enough and wanted to politely move on, or she might have been quite uncomfortable. Is her welfare compromised by being in a situation she decided she no longer wanted to be in? This is the critical question and we need to start looking at what kinds of outcomes F gets from these interactions. If having the autonomy to end the interaction is a successful strategy the vast majority of the time, and F continues to show interest in interacting with other dogs over the following months, then we can assume this is nothing to worry about. However, what if she starts to show a decline in her interest in other dogs?

Before we decide if this is worrying we should look at her age and experience. If she is socially maturing (12 months to four years, depending on the dog) she could be naturally losing interest in interacting socially with every dog she sees. If she is aging (over eight years old) or experiencing pain, it would also be typical to see a decline in her interest in other dogs. So, this on its own might not be indicative of how she is feeling. Another indicator might be how frequently she needs to escalate to more forceful requests for space. If it is happening often, we would expect to see her using the escalated signals more often than the 'Thanks, but no thanks' signals. Likewise, we would expect to see her escalate her signals if she found even this example of successful coping unpleasant, as that might help her avoid the other dog more quickly. We might also expect to see her rushing to her escalated signals even if the other dog hasn't yet invaded her space. This would tell us that Dog F is starting to anticipate an unpleasant event she would like to avoid if possible. She could even start to get more aroused the moment she steps into the park, or show less enthusiasm for walks if she goes to the park most times she leaves home. Monitoring changes in her behaviour and looking for signs of avoidance or increased sensitivity to a particular event will tell us how that event is affecting her long-term mood. Just like humans, dogs can become hostages of their own emotional state. Tracking behaviour will reveal how your dog's emotional state might be changing, and we do well to pay attention to this.

6

WHAT FLOATS YOUR DOG'S BOAT?

HOW CAN WE TELL IF A NEW SENSATION OR ACTIVITY IS GOING TO TICKLE A NAIVE DOG'S FANCY?

By now we have learned what dogs generally enjoy and what should float their boat. However, every dog is an individual and they don't come to us having encountered every experience that's available in life. Can we predict what young dogs will come to enjoy and what will never really do much for them?

The answers to these questions are valuable to dog owners for two reasons. Firstly, helping our dogs find new activities to enjoy introduces new reinforcers into their lives. Optimistic dogs have frequent access to reinforcers, so the more reinforcers that are available to them, the more opportunities they have to get positive outcomes from life. Furthermore, as dog owners, we can use reinforcers to reward behaviours that we like, want and need. The more reinforcers we know about, the more flexibility we have in cultivating valuable and desirable behaviours. The second, perhaps more obvious, reason is that it is tremendous fun to watch our dogs enjoying themselves. All the day's worries and anxieties can magically melt away when you are watching your dogs doing what they love to do.

This chapter will guide you in future explorations with your dog, understanding what motivates her, what canine desire and motivation

Finding out together what your dog enjoys
is rewarding for both humans and dogs.

look like, and how arousal can affect motivation. It will also touch on the role of breed in what motivates individuals, and how to find new activities your dog is particularly likely to enjoy.

Novelty is a double-edged sword

Our dogs are likely to encounter new objects, activities or environments and many of these can present a conundrum. They might provide an opportunity for access to reinforcers, but then again, they could turn out to be threatening or unpleasant. The naïve dog doesn't know, because they're new to him. With each new encounter, he might show his uncertainty with hesitance, or by approaching and retreating repeatedly. This approach-and-retreat dance is one that many animals display in the face of a novel object. They approach to investigate a potential source of resources, and retreat to avoid a potential source of threat. Keeping their initial investigations brief and then retreating is a safer way to explore than simply shoving their face, with all its vulnerable features, into close and prolonged proximity with a new object of unknown origin (which is not to say that is a strategy dogs never choose).

You can help your dog with these explorations by interacting with the novel object yourself. Research shows that when dogs are uncertain, they may take cues from familiar humans. If their human appears comfortable and relaxed and curious, the dogs can be reassured and find more courage to investigate. However, this social referencing can go both ways, and it's also possible that owners can transmit their own fear to their dog. Tension in your body during thunderstorms, or when strange dogs approach, might be telling your dog that there is danger nearby.

Owners can also inadvertently create conflict through the social pressure of trying to coax a dog to interact with a novel object. The dog might want to approach the owner but, equally, might want to avoid the new thing the owner is interacting with. He can't do both, so could become agitated and that's unlikely to help him. If the owner backs off from the object a little and encourages the dog to approach them at a safer distance from the potential threat, this might reduce some of the conflict. Some dogs may be so sensitive to social pressure that it's better to simply let them go back and forth while watching calmly and providing a safe base to retreat to. Research shows that, depending on the style of attachment they have with their humans, dogs treat their owners as a secure base from which to explore, similar to the way small children use their parents.

'Drive', arousal, motivation and persistence

A popular term among some dog trainers is 'drive'. The word probably has its origins in so-called 'drive-reduction theory', first proposed by American psychologist Clark Hull and based on the principle that all individuals possess core drives (for example: hunger, thirst and safety). Performing behaviours that achieve these goals is expected to reduce drive: the individual will learn to perform the behaviours because that drive reduction acts as an innate reinforcer. Drive-reduction theory was enticingly simple but fell out of favour because it could not explain secondary reinforcers (stimuli that can become reinforcing in themselves through their association to other reinforcers). It also struggles to explain why animals will create or maintain tension through the approach-and-retreat dance even when they are neither hungry nor thirsty, nor appear to have another drive that needs to be satisfied. Just as humans and other animals engage in behaviours that can put them in danger yet serve no primary goal (such as riding on rollercoasters), dogs will engage with novelty for no obvious primary drive-reduction purpose.

It is tempting to assume that if animals appear motivated to engage in activities that don't directly help them obtain resources, then there must be some other drive in play instead. Suddenly we have terms such as 'ball drive' to describe a dog's innate desire to play ball. Others might term this 'prey drive', assuming that the dog is performing a chase behaviour that would form part of a predatory sequence. Others refer to it as 'play drive', assuming that the behaviour is exclusively playful in nature. These assumptions make for difficult communication, and also fail to explain why chasing a ball just once is not sufficient to address the drive. We could argue that the dog simply has a lot of 'ball drive' to be satisfied, but then we are stuck with circular reasoning: the only way we can tell that a dog has 'a lot of ball drive' is because it chases a lot of balls. (Please note that we refer to balls for chasing: we never throw sticks for dogs because of the risk of catastrophic throat and mouth injury.)

That the concept of drive reduction persists suggests that people need a way to talk about a dog's level of motivation to attain a particular reinforcer, the dog's persistence in trying to obtain it, and how aroused they get when working at it. 'Drive' may be an attempt to combine those three concepts (arousal, motivation and persistence) into one descriptor, just as humans who are said to be 'driven' pursue their goals with relentless energy, motivation and persistence.

There can be many ways in which dog trainers use the word 'drive', so to avoid barking up the wrong tree or relying on circular reasoning, we will instead focus on the three core characteristics of a dog engaged in a given activity: arousal, motivation and persistence. Understanding how each of these influences the dog's behaviour and what they find reinforcing in any single moment will help us all work with our dogs rather than against them. This critical trinity helps us to capitalise on reinforcers in training and also explains how we can help dogs overcome some of their fears and phobias. As an added bonus, they can be measured independently of each other and of any particular reinforcer, thus we can avoid circular reasoning as well. Ah, the thrill and satisfaction of operating free of logical fallacies!

Ready, set, GO!

Arousal refers to a state of readiness to act. The dog who has managed to convince us to pick up a ball and is tense, staring fixedly at that ball, or dancing, maybe barking, and bouncing in anticipation of chasing it, is in a highly aroused state. That means she is ready to burst into action at any moment.

Arousal can be thought of as a ladder, with escalating rungs at an appropriate level of arousal for different activities. Research from the early 1900s conducted by Robert M. Yerkes and John Dillingham Dodson found a remarkable relationship between arousal and performance in rodents, which became known as the Yerkes–Dodson law. When tasks are easy, the higher the rats' arousal levels, the better they performed. However, when tasks are more difficult, performance increases with arousal to a certain point, but beyond that point, more arousal is associated with a decline in performance. As an example, imagine you are a parent on a school-day morning: the school bus is due in 10 minutes and no one who is meant to go to school is ready to do so. Children need to be dressed, lunches prepared, teeth cleaned and bags packed. Your heart pounds as you race against time, rushing around the house, throwing clothes at children and food from the fridge into lunchboxes, yelling about the pivotal role of dental hygiene in future corporate success. The more your heart pounds, the faster you can move, the more focused you are on the goal of getting everyone out of the house at 8.20am. Because this goal relies mainly on speed and single-minded focus, the more aroused you are, the more likely you are to attain it. In contrast, imagine you get the children out at 8.20am and then immediately sit down to compose an email to your boss while your heart is still pounding. It's hard to concentrate on the email when part of your brain is fretting about whether the kids appreciate the importance of travelling quickly and directly to the bus stop. Your partner turns up and helpfully stands at your shoulder to coach you in email composition by screaming: 'Come on, you yellow-bellied loser! What's another word for emotionally overwrought? Think! THINK!'

If only all that was needed to compose the perfect email to your superior was a bucket-load of arousal and a team coach ready to yell his throat raw. But it isn't — chiefly because the nature of arousal is that it is task-specific. Rather than speed and focus, writing requires you to sit still, sift through your thoughts to pull out the coherent ones, sift through your vocabulary for the words to express them, and construct it all into sentences that other people who cannot read your mind can understand. High arousal will result in struggling to concentrate. Conversely, too little arousal will result in being distractible and feeling like the whole thing is too hard right now. In contrast, moderate arousal will grant you the attention required to get the job done.

Unrealistic expectations

So, how do we relate this to our dogs and what makes them happy? We perform best when we are appropriately aroused for the task, and so do our dogs. Physically active endeavours, such as running and tugging, might not appear remotely attractive to a dog that is currently experiencing low arousal, but they could be extremely appealing to a

Sitting still requires lower arousal than running. A dog might not be able to switch easily from running to sitting.

dog who's been cooped up inside all day and is ready to expend energy after being sedentary for several hours. Likewise, if we want our dogs to pay attention to us and do what we ask, we should consider if they are suitably aroused for that activity.

Asking a dog to sit quietly to greet us when we come home, when he hasn't seen us all day, is like asking a toddler who is hurtling around the house to sit down and eat his lunch. His current arousal level is too high for him to easily perform that behaviour. The dog might manage to get his butt down, but will bounce to his feet again at the slightest provocation, such as when we happen to make eye contact. He is not showing any lack of obedience or respect for your authority. He is simply telling you that this behaviour is deeply unsuited to his current arousal level and he is having a hard time performing it. What's more, it pays to appreciate how an apparently easy behaviour can be more difficult than it appears — owners of greyhounds can relate to this well, because many of these dogs find lying down far easier than sitting.

For a dog to greet other dogs might appear a fairly easy task; one he should be able to perform, therefore, even when highly aroused. This is not the case! Strange dogs are a package of unknowns. Throughout their lives, dogs learn and refine different styles of communication and can use signals with varying degrees of subtlety. It takes brain power for a dog to detect and interpret all those signals, some of which might be unfamiliar or ambiguous, and then decide how he should respond in order to attain potentially competing goals, such as interacting with the new dog while also avoiding an aggressive response. A highly aroused dog will almost certainly miss signals from an unfamiliar dog. This can lead to a frequently seen pattern: the dog appears to want to

Navigating stairs with all those legs takes concentration!
Concentration needs lower arousal.

approach other dogs and even greets them politely at first, but then becomes liable to snap. Because he is too aroused to properly read other dogs, he finds they are often unpredictable and that interactions with them are fraught with danger. He snaps because he anticipates the interaction going bad at any moment; or he has detected a signal he's interpreted to mean that now is when the interaction is going bad, and he's buying space fast by going on the offensive to prevent being on the receiving end.

Just do it!

Arousal is a physiological state (heart rate, neurotransmitters, hormones flying in all directions) but motivation refers to having and achieving goals. It's probably a stretch to say that dogs wake up every morning and set themselves a list of goals. Indeed, there's no evidence that non-human animals have the foresight to plan a specific goal ahead of time as we do. (Although there is evidence that some animals, particularly corvids and perhaps primates, might be able to plan, by saving tools or food they do not want now but anticipate needing in the future. Dogs are not traditionally the mental heavyweights that corvids and primates are, but they have not been tested for this ability to plan.) However, most animals don't need to plan ahead: their lives revolve around obtaining resources when those resources are available, and seeking out those resources when they are not. In these endeavours, animals frequently engage in goal-directed behaviours that serve the function of finding and/or obtaining resources.

Scientists can measure motivation in animals by imposing a cost on particular resources or activities. We can measure an animal's motivation by the efforts they are willing to make to obtain the resource: how far they will travel for it, or how fast, or how high they will jump, or how much weight they will push to get to it. You can try this yourself with your own dog. For example, how many cushions can you pile on top of your dog's ball before he decides it's too hard to get to the ball? You could also try hiding the ball. How long will he search for it before he gives up? This can work with food treats as well. How distracting are they from other options? How quickly will he return to you when he knows they are on offer?

One word of warning, though: it pays to remember that dogs are learning all the time. If you hide goodies and encourage your dog to find them, he will get better and better at unearthing them. His success might also encourage him to persist longer in the future, and this makes it difficult to know whether he puts in more effort because he is more motivated, or because he has learned it usually pays off. These sorts of games are good mental stimulation for dogs, but it's wise to have a signal such as 'All done' which means the game is over, so your dog learns when to stop searching. Training your dog to switch off with an 'All done' signal makes life more bearable when you own a determined canine companion. You can think of this as the shop shutting; it's no longer open for business, no matter how much one might knock at the door. It's a tip that's good for owners and for their dogs; ball-chasers will run themselves into the ground and even make themselves vomit if they don't have such an off switch. (Nev and Bundy know that when Paul says this and shows them the palms of his two empty hands, the shop is officially shut.)

What to do when your dog doesn't know when to quit

Some dogs are persistent to a maddening degree. If you have one of those dogs who spends an hour trying to reach a toy you've put out of their reach, you could be blessed or cursed. 'Blessed' because such dogs can be very forgiving to train. If you are interested in dog sports, where rewards might not be allowed in the ring, the persistent dog is for you. 'Cursed' because they don't switch off that persistence when you want them to stop trying to reach the reinforcer you don't want them to have. Managing these dogs takes consistency and some dedication. If a dog learns that he needs only try hard enough for long enough to get what he wants, then you could find you have created a dog that can outlast you on just about anything. The ensuing battle of wills can consume enormous amounts of time; a commodity dogs have plenty of and most owners crave. Dogs can bark and whine at you longer than you can ignore them. They can keep putting a toy in your hand/coffee/clean laundry more times than you can cope with moving it (without throwing it for them and thus rewarding them). They rejoice in your attention to the object, the activity and to them.

If you mean to discourage problematic behaviour by making sure the dog isn't rewarded for it, you'd better be absolutely certain you can a) prevent him getting what he wants, even by accident; and b) ignore his infuriating behaviour for longer than he can persist with it. The key is to pick your battles and train a default behaviour. For example, training the dog to sit or lie down quietly as a way to 'ask' for whatever he wants, can go a long way towards minimising the number of obnoxious, yet effective, behaviours he discovers. Another trick is to train him to distance himself from you before every meal is placed on the ground.

Satiation and disinterest

We touched earlier on the role of arousal in performance and what happens when the dog in front of you lacks sufficient arousal for the task at hand. Arousal and interest are related so, if arousal is very low, we could find our dog is disinterested in engaging in an activity. This is most likely seen at times of the day when a dog is usually restful. Her arousal is low when she's napping for long periods, so asking her to get up and work with you could result in her being slow, easily distracted, prone to wandering off and failing to respond with her usual promptness and reliability. Just when you want to show off your dog's new trick to friends, she will give you a droll look, wag her tail gently and go back to bed. Of course, some dogs are ready to rock and roll at any time: it might be that they are difficult to satiate, or they are highly active.

Satiation is when an animal has had enough of a particular resource or activity that they don't want or need any more. We have all eaten so many chocolates or chips at one time that we just couldn't eat any more of them; we're said to be sated. It is fair to say we would still work for such party treats at a later time, so their reinforcing properties are only temporarily lost. Likewise, a dog who gradually loses interest in performing for a particular reinforcer might well work for that reinforcer another time. However, if every time we ate party treats, we ate them until we couldn't eat any more, it's possible we could lose interest in them altogether over time. They are no longer special, so their value has been depleted. Furthermore, we start to associate feeling satiated with the situations in which it occurs, and then those situations can on their own contribute to our losing interest in party treats. In other words, if you always train your dogs until they lose interest and wander off, they will reliably value working with you less.

One way to detect the difference between impending satiation and low arousal is to increase the rate of reinforcement. For example, if you are using treats, grab a small handful and aim to use them all up in reinforcing your dog's behaviour in under 20 seconds. Dogs often get more excited when the rewards are coming thick and fast. Think of driving on a main road where every set of lights turns green on your approach. Oh, the elation! Everything is going your way! However, if you have been driving on a deserted highway and every traffic light is green by default, you quickly lose interest in traffic lights. This is the result of satiation, not low arousal. Establish how quickly your dog perks up when you increase the rate of reinforcement: if he seems disinterested after you've increased reinforcement then he's most likely sated. If he becomes more engaged, you know you've boosted his arousal levels.

Born this way

Dogs were bred for many different purposes, and some breeds have been selectively bred for specific jobs over many generations. These outcomes are reflected in the so-called breed standards, which specify what a dog of a given breed must look like and, rather briefly and often vaguely, how it should behave. How much does breed purpose affect the activities that individual dogs are most motivated to perform? The short answer is that we don't know. That said, we do know that breeds that perform certain tasks often look the same. For example, the sight-hounds have long noses and the terriers often have short legs. This observation led us to examine the behavioural reports of owners of different breeds and consider how the overall make-and-shape of a dog can predict its behavioural tendency. What we discovered was fascinating but may not surprise the avid dog watcher. Some of the findings are easier to explain than others.

Short-skulled dogs were significantly more likely to show compulsive staring, self-grooming, allo-grooming (grooming of other dogs) and dog-directed aggression. And they were much less likely to be reported for food-stealing, stranger-directed fear, persistent barking and chasing moving objects.

Try engaging your dog with more frequent rewards if she ever seems disinterested.

Short-legged dogs were significantly more likely to show urination when left alone, defecation when left alone, separation-related problems and attention seeking. They were also more likely to show dog-directed fear, owner-directed aggression and touch sensitivity. They were also more likely to roll in faeces and mark with urine. These two findings might reflect that shorter dogs are closer to the ground and are more likely to encounter ground-based odours that can prompt these two behaviours. The list for these guys goes on. They were also more likely to beg for food, mount persons or objects, and chase shadows and lights. In addition, they were less trainable than their taller counterparts.

Lighter dogs were significantly more likely to show dog rivalry (perhaps because they have learned how vulnerable they are to being disposed from resources). Their light frames could explain why they tend to show more energy, excitability, hyperactivity and escaping or roaming.

Breeding dogs for certain purposes has favoured certain body shapes. It makes sense to consider that selectively breeding dogs to perform a particular job well should also include selectively breeding them to be particularly motivated to perform that job. However, the percentage of dogs that still perform the jobs they were originally bred for is generally quite small today. For some behavioural traits, a dog's temperament is influenced more by whether it was bred from show dogs or working dogs than what breed exactly it is. That said, this effect may be specific to certain regions. Our own research on Australian dogs shows a clear difference in behaviour between working line dogs and show line dogs, but also shows that breed can, to a small degree, predict personality traits.

It can be tough being short. Short dogs are more prone to attention-seeking behaviour.

There are many purebred individuals in the dog population who do not behave as the breed standard suggests they should, although breed standards are often brief when it comes to temperament, and it is hard to behave like a single sentence. There are more and more dog sports emerging that aim to provide dogs with opportunities to perform some of the behaviours they were originally bred to perform. Herding breeds can participate in herding competitions, sporting breeds can compete in retrieving or dock-diving (jumping off a dock into water), sight-hounds can participate in lure-coursing competitions, terriers can be involved in barn hunts (finding, but not harming, rodents in makeshift barns) or earthdog competitions (finding prey scents in artificial tunnels) and there are also mushing, canicross (cross-country running with dogs) and weight-pull sports for dogs that excel at pulling, and tracking or nose-work competitions for dogs to use their outstanding sense of smell. Traditional dog sports, such as obedience, agility and flyball, can be enjoyable for all breeds, but the breeds bred to work closely with humans tend to excel.

Participating in breed-specific sports as a way to make our dogs happy is not necessarily the only way we can give them the chance to participate in activities that reflect their distant origins. For example, breeds that traditionally worked in close association with humans seem to be extremely versatile, and many are delighted to embrace any activity their human sees fit to share with them. We might do best by our dogs to give them opportunities to find enjoyment in many activities and observe which ones they seem to like best. The key here is to pay close attention to what the dog is telling you. The *doglogbook* helps you to monitor the activities your dogs engage in and to estimate the joy they get from different forms of busyness.

Herding dogs often enjoy working with livestock,
but there are many other activities they can enjoy.

KESTREL THE EXPLORER

Melissa can tell that young Kestrel is highly motivated to explore her environment, because she starts screaming when the car stops (presumably in case anyone forgets to get her out) and won't get back in the car at the end of a walk without significant bribery — unless she's been for a good 10 kilometre (6 mile) run. After that, she is sufficiently satiated with exploration to willingly come home. Kestrel's very high motivation for exploration is also manifested by how difficult it is to divert her from this activity. Many and frequent rewards were necessary to train her to pay attention to her humans to the point where she could forsake her explorations to return when called. Virtually any environment that is not the backyard is exciting for Kestrel. This is true of many dogs and helps to explain why having a (large) backyard is never an antidote to canine boredom or frustration.

We can more fully understand Kestrel's motivation to explore if we look at what she finds in her explorations and how she responds to them. She follows her nose to track down the source of smells, which she then either eats in a ridiculously short time or rolls on for a ridiculously long time. She gets particularly excited if her movements provoke insects or small animals to flee. She comes alive and increases the speed of her explorations and suddenly starts ranging far and wide. If she flushes out more critters, her excitement soars again and she might start barking. She rushes to investigate the source of any unusual sound, smell or movement. Her breed (the Portuguese podengo pequeno) was bred to flush rabbits from difficult terrain, so it's perhaps unsurprising that, compared to other dogs, she seems hyper-focused on directionless exploring — we can hypothesise about what activities we could give her to tickle that exploratory nature without flushing rabbits. She will probably excel at games that require her to follow sudden movements or to use her nose to find rewards. She is always shifting quickly to the next stimulus, so if we want her to persist with activities, we might need to reward her frequently and in surprising ways to keep her interest.

We can also see what activities our dogs are particularly motivated to do by what happens when they don't get to perform them. As a young dog, Kivi became very restless and mouthy — both signs of frustration — if he had not played with other dogs for a few days. Although this sort of mouthing is often a cause of questions to trainers and vets, and sometimes even of early surrendering to shelters, stopping it is sometimes simply a matter of understanding why it is occurring: frustration is a common cause. Social frustration is not a problem that the owner of every young dog faces. Some dogs seem to want more social interaction than others. Erik loves to engage with his humans, and becomes increasingly demanding the longer he goes without a good training session. His activity of choice is trick training, although this is probably because Melissa's training goals of choice are tricks. Erik is one of those versatile working dogs who will throw himself into any activity his humans feel like doing.

Match your skill sets

It pays to consider these historic roles if your heart is set on a pedigree dog. Pick a variety that was bred to have skills that are manageable in your household and lifestyle. It is possible, but rather unlikely, that to be truly happy, some individual dogs need to participate in activities that align with their breed's original purpose. Of course, many dogs are not doing anything related to that historic function but are still having enriching lives. And many crossbred dogs can have mixed ancestry that defies attempts to guess a specific preferred activity. The purpose of this discussion is simply to inspire you to think about the kinds of activities your dog might particularly enjoy. Likewise, think carefully about this before committing to a breed. Australian kelpies were bred to work with livestock for long hours on rural holdings. When we put GPS collars on the kelpies working on one of Sydney University's farms, we were amazed to find some regularly cover over 65 km (40 miles) per day. Is this an appropriate dog to live in a townhouse while you work 10 hours a day? Urban living might work with some individuals, but equally, they might be rare. Siberian huskies are beautiful dogs, but they were bred to pull sleds up to 40 km (25 miles) a day in snow and ice and they tend to be interested in killing small animals. Is this a suitable breed for your suburban garden in the sub-tropics that is shared with chickens and guinea pigs?

Breed tendencies are just that — tendencies. Occasional individuals might fit in conditions we couldn't imagine them suited to, but generally there will be trouble if you get an active working breed but don't intend to work with it or exercise it adequately. And the more that lack of exercise frustrates a dog, the more feral their behaviour can become. This begins a vicious circle of confinement, hyperactivity and unruly behaviour that all too often sends dogs spiralling down to shelters and premature euthanasia. We hope that for dedicated dog owners spending quality time with their dogs, exercising, training and going fun places together, this would be an unthinkable outcome.

Active dogs can make great exercise buddies,
but make sure you will have the time for it.

7

HOW TO BE YOUR DOG'S BEST FRIEND

HUMANS DON'T SPEAK THE SAME LANGUAGE AS DOGS.

We are verbal, and travel on two legs, leaving our hands free to manipulate our world; clearly, this is dramatically different to how dogs go about their lives, and presents a challenge to both dogs and humans to understand one another. Dogs are often interested in what humans are doing. This could be because we give them many valued resources, but some studies suggest that dogs are born inherently more interested in humans than wild canids will ever be. Given that we are surrounded by such eager sponges for information, we owe it to our dogs to help by being consistent and predictable. This makes us easier to understand, easier to read and easier to have fun with. Despite what might be a natural gift in our dogs for communication with humans, they do not come boxed-and-ready to read our minds; they have plenty to learn about the signals used by their own species as well. We should take a moment to appreciate the task ahead of them in learning the different, sometimes baffling, signals of another species.

We can meet our dogs halfway in their efforts to understand us, by doing our best to be readily understandable. Let's face it, we might be the ones with hefty forebrains, but when it comes to body language, dogs are doing the heavy lifting in dog–human relationships. Dogs can communicate volumes to each other with a mere look that leaves us humans mystified. We can help our dogs with their communication

Dogs are experts at deciphering our body language,
but we can help them out by being consistent and clear.

efforts by paying attention to what they are signalling and endeavouring to respond appropriately to those messages. We can assist them in obtaining or changing their goals, depending on whether those goals are safe and appropriate. Humans are excellent at empathy and emotional intelligence and we can use these to help us be our dog's best friend. This chapter will look at situations in which communication between dogs and humans flourishes and where it flounders, and easy remedies for communication breakdowns.

Your body is semaphore for your dog

We have discussed that dogs are not a visual species in the same way that humans are, but they are even less a verbal species. Humans naturally verbalise when communicating, no matter who or what we are communicating with. We even talk to inanimate objects. How many times have you attempted to sweet-talk a computer or car? We emote with words, while dogs communicate with visual signals, so they are already primed to pay attention to where our hands are, how the shape of our bodies change predictably in association with certain events, where our centre of mass is, what we're looking at, and how we move.

This is great for us because, although dogs may struggle to make sense of our nouns, adjectives and verbs, a puppy comes to us understanding some basic body language that holds across species.

Hands hold answers

There is a sizeable body of literature from canine science laboratories in Europe on dogs following human pointing. The latest reports suggest that dogs are supremely interested in pointing because hands reliably deliver so many reinforcers. If you give your dog treats from your hand, hands become associated with treats. But, to dogs, hands are associated with far more than just food rewards. You carry your dog's food bowl in your hands, you stroke your dog with your hands and rub their belly, you pick up the all-important car keys with your hands, you put on the leash with your hands, and you throw balls and play tug with your hands. Hands are the bearers of many wonderful reinforcers and are well worth a dog's scrutiny and attention. We can trade on this by using our hands to guide dogs into positions.

You might have learned in puppy school to put a treat in your hand and then lift your hand up in front of your dog's nose. Your dog follows the movement of your hand and sits so she can more easily tilt her head up towards the treat. When the head goes up, the butt (generally) goes down.

So, hands can cue a dog's head to move relative to her butt, but can also be used to move the dog from one spot to another. All of this is known as luring, and we can use it to lead dogs through many behaviours, over obstacles, onto platforms and into spaces. Imagine there is an invisible string that operates when your hand is about 20 cm (8 inches) away from your dog's nose. Too close and the dog will lunge forwards to try to reach your hand, but too far away and she won't follow the movement. Likewise, if you move your hand too slowly, she will probably move towards it to get the treat, but if you move it too quickly, she will lose track of it. When the speed of movement and the distance are just right, the luring effect of your hand is almost magical.

Many of us rely on our dominant hand to guide our dogs and they too become attentive to just one hand. This is a trap that the best trainers avoid. As an exercise, it is worth testing how agile and effective you can be with both left and right hands. Becoming ambidextrous in this sense can effectively double your chances of communicating with clarity.

You can use this knowledge of the invisible string to troubleshoot if you are ever having trouble using luring to get your dog to perform a behaviour. Play around with the distance you are using throughout the movement of your hand, and the speed with which you move your hand. If you still can't find a sweet spot, think about what your dog is doing instead of what you want her to do, and how you can adjust the path of your hand to help her understand. For example, if she is not getting the hang of following your hand into a *down*, look at where her nose is going. If she is putting her nose close to her front paws and remaining in a standing or seated position, you may need to move your hand back towards her chest where she can't reach it so easily from her current position.

Conversely, moving your hand out towards or beyond her front paws may do the trick if she is tall or heavy or otherwise reluctant to walk forwards and hang her head when she could reach forwards from a lower position. You can also try twisting your hand to one side of her to get her to roll onto her hip. Then if we want her to roll over from a down position, we want her nose to swing in an arc down towards her chest and then over her shoulder.

SHAPING BEHAVIOUR

Trainers use a process called 'shaping' to train an animal to perform new behaviours by reinforcing successive approximations of it. In other words, think of what the behaviour would look like if you animated it by capturing several frames. Shaping is where you reinforce each frame. Giving your dog rewards for small steps in the process will keep her interested, but avoid rewarding her only for

Many dogs have learned to pay a lot of attention to hands — the bearers of many good things.

the basic first steps lest she trains you to expect no more than that. And always choose a comfy surface, such as sand or a carpet, for this early training. A shiny, slippery surface can put a dog off this response for a long time. Keep watching the speed of your hand, the distance between your hand and her nose, and the path of your hand and note how small changes to any of these can affect how she moves in response.

Sometimes hands can signal negative outcomes, such as being grabbed, dragged, pulled, captured, lifted, restrained or even struck. Some dogs may become shy of the human hand and learn to avoid it because it is more often associated with events they don't like. Other dogs may learn to baulk, particularly when hands are outstretched towards them, or open or moving quickly. Still other dogs need no prior negative experiences to duck or scuttle backwards when a hand comes near their face. It pays to appreciate that a hand is often the first part of a human to invade a dog's space. In general, it is helpful to have a dog that moves towards your hand, regardless of what your hand is doing. Target training (training your dog to place his nose on your hand) can help with this, especially if you honour the dog's trust by never grabbing him or giving him any aversive outcome after he has targeted your hand. With cautious dogs, this training can save lives. For example, when luring a dog away from danger, such as poisonous or very hot objects.

Any time spent developing a dog's trust in your hands is always time well spent. When you need to get your dog on a leash urgently for his own safety — and you forget to take it slowly and lunge for his collar

Dogs will follow food in your hand, allowing you to guide them into different positions and then reward them.

— that is the moment it most pays to have a dog that sees hands as deliverers of positive outcomes.

If you do have a dog that is a little shy of hands, either sometimes or often, work on this by practising having your dog move into your hands. Crouch down, hold treats in one hand, low and near your body, hold your other hand out a little closer to the dog, then call your dog in. Show him the treats, if need be. As he approaches your treat hand, slowly move your other hand up beside his shoulder and gently place it on his collar. Always treat him for allowing this innocuous contact. You're essentially training him to press his collar into your non-treat hand. The more you practise this, the more backwards pressure you can put on his collar, and the faster you can move the hand without the treats. Trainers who practise this regularly soon end up with dogs that see an outstretched hand (as opposed to one closed on an object, for example) and race to press their collar into it. Handy! But remember to double your effectiveness by ensuring that both hands become equally trustworthy and attractive to your dog.

Centre of mass makes a difference

Your centre of mass is the point where your body's mass is most concentrated (not its centre of gravity, which is where the average weight of an object resides, and that is dependent on gravitational forces). Centre of mass is usually considered to be just below and behind your navel when you are standing, but it changes depending on how you move. If you crouch, your centre of mass is much lower. If you bend over, it travels forward, as the weight of your torso shifts ahead of your navel. Your centre of mass can predict how stable you are and in which direction you can most easily move. When you are

Shy dogs are more likely to approach if you crouch and offer a hand at your side, rather than in front of you.

standing upright you can move in any direction, but it's easier to move forwards, backwards or sideways than it is to move up and down. When you are bent over it's easy to go forwards and down, but going backwards is much harder, because your centre of mass is ahead of your hips, which is where you generate the movement required to go backwards. If you then lift your torso by straightening your back, your centre of mass starts to move back towards your hips, making backwards movement come more easily. If you are crouched, your centre of mass is low and you are pretty stable. You can lean in all directions without much trouble, but moving requires either an explosive lunge forwards or maybe sideways, or some awkward crab walking as you try to manage legs that are not designed for crouching locomotion. We don't know exactly how much of this dogs understand, but we can often see a change in how closely a dog will approach us if we change our centre of mass.

If you are low to the ground and someone is leaning towards you with their centre of mass forwards of their feet, the most likely direction they will move is down on top of you. If you are the slightest bit worried that they might crush or capture you, then that is a threatening posture. Standing upright is less threatening, but the size difference between dogs and humans means that a human still looms over towards a dog if they mean to make contact. A crouching human is less threatening than a looming one. The crouching human is much lower to the ground and therefore closer to the dog. If the human leans forwards, he will remain quite stable.

As body language experts, dogs know how to remain safe around bipedal primates. Many dogs have learned that crouching humans are unlikely to make sudden movements. The harder it is for you to move

Leaning away from your dog and moving
backwards quickly invites him to follow.

suddenly towards a dog, the less threatening you look. So adopting a more upright position or even leaning backwards as a way to invite a dog to approach, is saying 'Hey, I'm woefully unprepared to grab you. That's how safe I am.' Now you might notice how aloof-looking humans seem to receive more unsolicited boisterous canine greetings than looming humans.

Remember these tricks, even if you have a dog that usually wants to be close to you. If they are keeping their distance for some reason, you can encourage them to come in by running backwards (carefully!) away from them. A backwards jog aligns your body in an angle away from the dog, and you're also moving away from them while still facing them. It's inviting to many dogs. A word of caution, remember that you are easier to topple backwards in this posture! A dog that is excited by this new game might jump up and manage to push you above your centre of mass, and there's a good chance that his mass and momentum will push you off balance. That's physics, folks!

Speed and movement are attention grabbers!

Objects that move quickly around dogs tend to excite them. Whether that is because the movement reminds them of small critters or livestock, running away from them, or whether it's because fast-moving objects are unpredictable and perhaps threatening, movement will capture the attention of many dogs. They usually learn over time that some fast-moving objects (cyclists, skateboarders, other dogs, vehicles, screaming children) are part of everyday life and not fun to chase. If, historically, a dog has been threatened by objects that move with speed, she may have learned that many of them (for example, flies) seem to disappear when chased and, even though this might have happened anyway by chance, this reward can be enough to keep her on the job.

That probable relevance of movement to dogs often provokes a spike in arousal associated with capturing a dog's focus. What happens then? He is very likely to perform some kind of energetically costly behaviour — typically, chasing the moving object. He might not notice peripheral stimuli (for example, you calling his name) so it can be difficult to get him to respond to you. An unresponsive dog chasing a moving object can obviously be a big problem. If he doesn't notice you calling him, he is also unlikely to notice signs that he is in great danger. It is natural for him to be excited by movement and then ignore you while he pursues it — although this may not be terribly reassuring when you are in fear of your dog being killed by a car, causing injury to an innocent bystander or getting you publicly shamed. It may help you think of ways to get his attention in the first place, though.

If your dog's interest in you is lukewarm or he is distracted, moving faster is likely to arouse him, his interest will blossom, his ears will come up and forward and his eyes will brighten — and he might just respond the way you were trying to get him to respond all along. You can move faster yourself, or you can grab a toy and try whipping that around. It's best to retain control of it rather than throwing it and hoping your dog will go after it, though. Wait until he is fully focused on the toy and actively trying to grab it before you throw it for him.

Influencing the excitement level of dogs with their own enthusiasm is a skill that dog trainers often admire in others, but we are not just limited to revving up our dogs. It is an enviable skill to be able to reduce arousal if your dog is too excited. Slower movements are less arousing and can defuse a dangerously charged situation. Just breathing calmly seems to have a similar effect, which is of interest to anyone who rides horses. It has been shown that simply telling a rider she can expect an object to appear at a certain location is enough to send her horse's heart rate up and make it more reactive at that spot.

If your dog is excessively excited by moving objects, you can use distance from the objects and their speed to control the intensity of the stimulation and make it easier for your dog to focus on you instead. If fast cars on main roads provoke worrying levels of interest, try visiting a picnic ground with a car park. You can use the extra space afforded by a large open area and the slower speed of cars parking to help desensitise your dog to moving cars.

Winding up and winding down with sounds and touch

Dogs respond differently to sounds with different attributes. A short, sharp, moderately loud sound will tend to grab a dog's attention; Melissa likes to belt out 'Oi!' when she wants her dogs to stop what they are doing and look at her. Whatever attention-getting sound you choose will work even better if you pair it with food. A dog training 'clicker' (a simple plastic box with a metal tongue that can be held in your hand and clicked) is especially good for producing a short, sharp sound for working with your dog at close quarters. Whistles can be a good tool for recalling dogs over longer distances — the unusual, loud sound carries well and can be heard clearly over background noises in most environments. Nev and Bundy have been trained to listen out for their names being whispered on a walk, since this reliably heralds the promise of a treat if they return to Paul.

As we noted in Chapter 1, dogs are often responsive to high-pitched sounds. Squeaky toys tend to warrant excited investigation and making a huge fuss in a high-pitched voice when your dog has been a superstar for even just an instant will often provoke excited tail-wagging and wriggling. Exclamations like 'Oh my goodness, you're so clever; aren't you clever? Who's clever? Is it you? You? Are you the

Slow and gentle strokes and tickles can be very calming for a dog, and for the human as well.

clever one? YES, YOU ARE!' usually succeed in communicating positive excitement to a dog, unless they are particularly timid. Those seeking to boost their dogmanship will know that when it comes to verbal praise the tails have it. What you may think is a convincing display of enthusiasm on your part is of no importance if the dog in front of you is not wagging his confirmation.

Enthusiastic praise can be used to reinforce desired behaviour, but may also serve to arouse dogs to a level where speed or sharpness of performance will come easier. For example, starting a game of fetch or tug with 'Where's your toy? Where is it? Are you going to GET IT?' can help ensure your dog is in the mood to play. The short, sharp sentences can be uttered in exciting bursts. Sometimes changes in the speed of speech can encourage excited anticipation: 'Arrrre... yooooou... goiiiiiing... tooooo... GETIT?'

Vigorous physical contact, such as rubbing, pushing, patting and fast scratching can also be arousing to many dogs. Of course, not all dogs like this kind of contact and some might back off if you try it. This is important information for you: if you see your dog retreat a little, simply stop and wait for him to come to you to re-establish contact. If and when he does, be a bit gentler this time. Keep your play bout short and then stop to see if he comes right back for more. How fast he re-engages will tell you how much he enjoys what you just did. Be mindful that he might change what he likes from moment to moment. High-arousal play is best in short bursts and you can avoid leaving him hanging by lowering the arousal in your play in successive play bouts, so that by the time you are ready to end the games both you and your dog are much calmer.

Calming sounds are the opposite to arousing sounds. Long, slow, low-pitched noises, preferably quieter in volume, will often help dogs calm themselves. De-escalating touches should also be long and slow strokes or firm, massaging circles or a bit of both. Communicate your calmness by taking some deep breaths yourself.

Timing is about 33 per cent of everything

Timing is one of the three cornerstones of effective communication with any animal. The others are consistency and reinforcement. Assuming that x is the behaviour you want to reinforce, for your dog to learn that when she does x she gets y, y must follow immediately after x occurs. If there is a delay of a couple of seconds, she might have already gone on to perform behaviour z after x, or she could have been distracted by another stimulus, or be focused on what she is doing right now instead of what she did a moment ago. Thus, when y occurs, she will associate it with whatever is most immediately obvious to her.

This is why many good trainers use so-called 'markers', or 'bridges'. Markers are a way to tell an animal he's just earned reinforcement. They give trainers breathing room so that they don't have to somehow reinforce the animal when he is halfway through completing a behaviour, or when he is not close to the trainer. Trainers can signal with their choice of marker (for example: whistle or clicker, as mentioned earlier, 'Good', or even a flashing light) and because they always follow the marker with reinforcement, the animal comes to see the marker as a reinforcer itself. The relationship between a marker and a reinforcer is critical. A marker will lose its reinforcing properties if it is not paired with real reinforcement often enough. Likewise, with classical conditioning, the goal is for the dog to associate an outcome with a particular stimulus. He will have trouble making that connection if the relationship between stimulus (the marker) and outcome (the reward) are not strong and clear. The stimulus should predict the outcome, so if we want a shy dog to enjoy the company of unfamiliar people, when the dog sees a stranger, food appears in front of her nose. If instead, the dog sees a stranger, then she sees another dog in the distance and only then does food appear in front of her nose, she will make the association with the distant dog instead of the stranger. If she is sniffing the ground and food appears in front of her nose and then she notices a stranger, any helpful association is again corrupted. Does sniffing simply predict food? Either way, in her mind, the stranger didn't help the food appear.

Sent to the naughty corner?

The same timing problems apply to punishment. If your dog will not come when called, punishing him when he finally gets back serves to punish the last behaviour he performed. In the dog's mind, that was coming back to you, rather than failing to come when called. People often try to use a more gentle punishment, such as a time-out, with dogs, particularly with unruly puppies. The problem with a time-out is it takes time to move a puppy into the spot where she is supposed to have her time-out. Furthermore, moving puppies often involves touching them, which they like! For a time-out to be effective, it needs to be instant and clear. Some trainers advocate a different marker (such as: 'Too bad') and then immediately remove themselves instead of the puppy. This can solve the timing and unintended reinforcement problems, but the trainer needs to be able to remove herself quickly and without exciting the puppy. For this reason, we rarely recommend time-outs as a punishment. Additionally, puppies are babies and can get over-aroused just like any youngster. Pups that have offered an unwelcome behaviour generally benefit more from being encouraged to lie down and settle. This can be achieved with a chew item and some confinement somewhere safe, such as a pen or crate.

A time-out is a difficult negative consequence for a misbehaving puppy, because she will follow you.

Humans who are both new to and experienced in animal training often have trouble with timing, and all (humble/reflective) trainers admit that they can improve their timing. It is not just a matter of observation skills, but also being prepared to make quick decisions on whether the behaviour the animal just offered was close enough to the behaviour the trainer wants, and so should be reinforced. One way to practise technique without inflicting your poor timing on a dog is to toss a ball in the air and try to clap your hands just as it reaches its highest point and starts to descend. It is also great practice with a dog to shape small behaviours from scratch. Melissa shapes a rear paw lift as an exercise to sharpen her timing and observation skills. While Paul trains dogs to look away for increasing periods because, for a dog that wants to give you his undivided attention, it is a behaviour that ends very quickly if you're not quick enough to reinforce it.

Consistency is power

Some of the problems with poor timing can be overcome with consistency. For example, consider classical conditioning. If we are slow to deliver treats, or provide them early, the dog is not sure what predicted the treats. Maybe our timing isn't always perfect, but we might be able to fall back on more repetitions, making the process consistent enough that the dog learns anyway. Say we produce the treats too late 10 per cent of the time and we are too early 10 per cent of the time, the remaining 80 per cent we are consistent enough to allow the dog to make the association we want.

Consistency is about predictability. The more consistent you are, whether that be in the signals you use with your dog, how often you reinforce her, when and where you give your cues, the better she can predict what you are asking of her, and the more consistent she will be in her response.

Dogs are experts at details, which means they notice all the variations in how we ask them to perform behaviours. This can be confusing to them when one member of the family says 'down' and another says 'drop', both intending to cue the same behaviour. Melissa considers one step in training is to have her partner cue any new trick. Inevitably, the first time her partner tries, the dog will just stand there in bemusement. Why is this? Because Melissa cues consistently and the cue looks and/or sounds different to the way her partner issues it, even though her partner copies her.

As dogs get more practised at responding to a new cue, they learn all the tiny variations in the way that cue is presented, and thus learn to broaden their acceptance. Soon, any stranger off the street can give the cue and they know how to respond. This is called generalisation: the dogs choose to respond because they are consistently reinforced for doing so. There is often pressure on dog owners from observers to 'fade the treat' and have dogs perform cued behaviours without reinforcement. Some dogs start to respond habitually and 'good dog' and a chest scratch is enough to maintain that level of response. But there are numerous dogs out there who will simply respond less and less when they are reinforced inconsistently. This is completely normal across the animal kingdom and does not mean your dog doesn't love or respect you enough. He just doesn't find praise very reinforcing.

Being consistent can also come back and bite us if we're not careful. Often we hear from dog owners that their dog is very well behaved at obedience classes, but when asked to perform a behaviour outside class, the dog acts as if she's never heard of it. Or she will only perform it when the owner finds some treats to wave in front of her. This points to a dog who has learned to be obedient at obedience class, because that is the place they are consistently asked to perform these behaviours and consistently reinforced for performing them (or

punished for not performing them, depending on the class). Failing to respond unless food is present tells us the dog is using the presence of food as a good predictor of being reinforced and has learned that the context of the class is critical for her prediction to work. If we want our dog to perform behaviours on cue, reliably and everywhere, whether we have food in our hand or not, then we need to make sure we are consistent in cueing behaviours and reinforcing them EVERYWHERE we want the dog to perform the behaviour reliably. That is why showing your dog that you have a treat is an unwise practice. It can very easily train your dog to check you out for treats before responding. Your mantra is 'Training can happen anywhere and any time'. That is what we want the dog to believe and we can achieve that by applying the consistency we use in training to every context.

The right reinforcement in the right place at the right time

Consistency and good timing will get you a long way in training any animal, but you can refine your success even more by using reinforcement thoughtfully. First, pick the reward that will support your training goals. That means, think about arousal, and satiation in particular. If you want high arousal, try toy play as a reward. Fabric tug toys are perfect for this job because they can be carried out of sight, in a trouser pocket. But even a few seconds of tug or chase can be physically taxing, so be aware that you may have to reduce the number of behaviours you ask for, so that you don't risk your dog becoming too tired (sated) to play anymore. If you want low arousal, prolonged food rewards, such as licking (all-natural) peanut butter from a spoon works very well. (Dogs often develop the strategy of

A game of tug-of-war is an exciting reinforcer that increases your dog's arousal.

scraping a pile of peanut butter into their mouth in an instant. It is sensible to load a spoon with a small amount of gooey treat, if we want a dog to take their time with it.) Maybe you want moderate arousal, but lots of repetitions, and in that case very small food rewards can be tossed into a dog's mouth to be consumed in an instant. (If your dog does not have great eye–mouth coordination, or you throw like a drunken sloth, you can deliver treats directly to the dog's mouth.)

TREAT TRAINING FOR HUMANS

One perennial problem with using treats in training is that the animal can become a landshark and snatch or take your whole treat hand, or try to climb into your treat pouch/treat hand instead of being an attentive student. To combat this, first make sure you don't reinforce snatching or mugging! Keep the food firmly inside your palm with your fingers wrapped around it. You can keep a handful of treats there, and use your thumb to move them to the outer side of the middle of your index finger, as you wish to make them available to your dog. If attempts are made to pry more treats out of your hand, you can often just wait the dog out. If no treats are coming out, the dog will soon learn that this is not a good strategy. As soon as she gives up and backs off from your hand, give her a treat so that she learns mugging doesn't work, but waiting away from the hand does. If you have trouble managing a handful of treats without dropping them, you may have better luck using a treat pouch, or holding the treats in one hand and taking them out and delivering them one at a time. It's worth practising, though, because fast treat delivery improves timing and, therefore, your training success!

Treats fallen on the ground can distract a dog for a while, meaning you have to wait for him to finish foraging before you can do more training. You can use that to your advantage when you want to distract him, for example from a cat walking along a nearby fence.

Reward placement can also help you refine your training. When rewards are close to where you want the dog to be when he finishes the behaviour, then he is reinforced both for approximations that meet the standards you have set and for being where you want him at the end of the task. For example, you might be training your dog to stand. You don't want him to move into a stand and then take another step, so make sure his treats appear right where you want his head to be when he is standing. You can also use reward placement to help a dog make an association. He may learn to target an object with his nose more quickly if the reward appears in close proximity to (for example, on top of) the object you want him to target.

Training animals is as much art as science. We humans can learn to be better animal trainers if we pay attention to how small changes in our behaviour affects the behaviour of our dogs. There is a lot to consider, and a phone video recorder can be your best friend. But, even if all you care about is having your dog do what he's asked when he's asked in everyday life, communicating with him clearly will assist you in that goal.

8

DOGS ARE
SOCIAL
ACROBATS

OUR DOMESTIC DOGS ARE A TRULY WONDROUS SPECIES IN MANY WAYS.

Perhaps their most impressive characteristic is the ability to forge social harmony. And not just social harmony with their kin, but with members of their own species of various makes and shapes, who may be unrelated to them or of no particular importance to their own survival. Arguably more than any other species, dogs can create social harmony between different species, whether these are humans, cats, birds or others. The social environments dogs find themselves in vary considerably, from eking out an existence on the streets of developing countries, sharing and competing with other street dogs, to semi-feral states in more rural areas, working roles with humans, other dogs and potential prey species, to dearly loved companions of humankind.

These social environments create different pressures and forms of competition for them, yet they manage to orchestrate social harmony regardless of the distribution of resources, the personalities of other dogs they must live among, and the species they might share space with. Dogs' social flexibility is awe-inspiring in the animal world — perhaps approaching that of humans.

Nevertheless, there are limits to what dogs can achieve socially. This chapter will discuss those limits, how to approach socialising your dog and how to manage ongoing social interactions to help dogs exploit their social flexibility to its full extent.

It is truly remarkable that dogs who don't know each other can come together and co-exist in harmony.

Socialisation is a window, but being sociable is for life

A fantastic, large-scale scientific report on dog behaviour was published in the 1960s by John Paul Scott and John L. Fuller. (Decades later, it can be found in book form and, surprisingly, and rather sadly, nothing like it has been published since.) For dog owners, a key message of Scott and Fuller's work was the existence of a sensitive period for socialisation in puppies. Thanks to their meticulous studies, it is now common knowledge that puppies need to be exposed to stimuli they will encounter in everyday life while they are in their 'socialisation window' — a period of openness to new information that usually occurs around 3–12 weeks of age in domestic dogs. The period is shorter in wolves, which is thought to be an important aspect in how dogs and wolves differ. (Wolves are extremely sociable, yet also somewhat insular. They are exceptionally close to their own family, but outsiders to the group are often attacked.) Scott and Fuller's work prompted the gradual development of puppy socialisation programmes and, eventually, classes designed to take advantage of the sensitive socialisation period and expose puppies to as many important stimuli as possible. Having the puppy meet other puppies, adult dogs, other companion animals, humans of different shapes, sizes, ages and looks, and exposing them to handling and equipment such as collars and leashes is supposed to prime them for the life ahead of them.

We must never underemphasise how important socialisation is in priming dogs for a happy life. The more about life with us that they find normal or positive during this period, the easier it will be to take them out-and-about and expose them to forms of enrichment such as walks and play and holidays, and the more likely they are to enjoy this. The quality of the socialisation experience is easily as important as the number of encounters a puppy has during this period. It is critical that the puppy is not frightened or overwhelmed. That said, it would be a mistake to focus so much on the socialisation period that we forget about the rest of the dog's development and life. Dogs are learning throughout life, but the socialisation period is pivotal because it serves to lay the foundations on which we must continue to build.

The continual building throughout life means ensuring our dogs have positive or neutral experiences with stimuli we want them to accept. The socialisation window might close at around three months of age, but young dogs still have much to learn, particularly about the social signals of their own species. As they mature, dogs develop their own styles of communication, as do humans. The socialisation period can allow puppies to overcome fear of other dogs or humans if their interactions are positive, but only with experience do they learn how to 'speak dog'. The more well-socialised dogs they meet and interact with, the more socially adept they become. So, rather like herd immunity in the child vaccination debate, the need for socialising individuals is clear, but making as many dogs as sociable as possible is paramount because that can influence the safety of the whole population. The more socialisation is provided for all pups, the more peace will prevail among dogs in ensuing generations.

This is of critical importance because we are asking dogs to live with us in increasingly dense conurbations and to share smaller common spaces in towns and cities. We owe it to the dogs of the future to address causes of fear in all its forms, and appropriate and adequate socialisation is where that mission starts. That is why we have put so much thought into the socialisation suite of the *doglogbook* app.

A canine social
genius will adopt a
play style that his
playmates enjoy.

Wallflowers, social geniuses and party-goers

Not all dogs are happy to be the life of the party and interact with any dog in any style. Some dogs are wallflowers — easily frightened or overwhelmed, sometimes in spite of good socialisation. Allowing these dogs to approach others slowly, one dog at a time, and picking dogs for them to meet who are gentle, slow and predictable will set them up for success in their social interactions so that they gradually become more confident. Some dogs, for whatever reason, generally do not want to make friends with other dogs or humans. They should not be expected to just because it might suit us.

Other dogs are the veritable social geniuses of the dog world. They are enormously flexible and responsive in their social interactions. These dogs are often very motivated to interact with other dogs, but will adjust their behaviour to facilitate positive interactions. The social genius may largely ignore dogs who are wary; he might move slowly, allowing them to approach him when they gather the courage. And, then again, he will joyfully wrestle with dogs who like to wrestle, parallel run with dogs that prefer not to play contact sports, and flop on the ground to let smaller dogs climb on him or play with his face. He matches his energy level and play style to the dog he is interacting with. We can learn a lot from watching how he manages his social interactions with other dogs.

Party-goers are the boisterous, friendly dogs of the world who have never heard of personal space. A party-goer tends to flourish in dog parks where she can roar up and down with other dogs, running, wrestling and jostling. Of course, if she tries to interact with a more sensitive dog in this manner, she will probably find herself on the receiving end of some sharp, distance-increasing behaviours, such as a growl, snap or rush. And, if she irks another dog, they might 'start' a fight with her — although it was she who started it really, when she invaded their space so abruptly. Party-goers can be great dogs for suburban family settings: outgoing, sociable dogs, who are not remotely sensitive about their body space, may also be comparatively safe around children and other dogs. However, every owner bears the responsibility to avoid their dog upsetting other dogs (or humans, particularly children and less mobile adults) who do not want a 30 kg (5 stone) Labrador partying on their head. It is recommended to always maintain vigilance, a rock-solid recall and the starting assumption that a newcomer doesn't want to be instantly partied with.

More than just a dog owner

The modern dog in Western civilisation often mixes more with humans than with their own kind. The single urban or suburban dog living in a human family is the norm and, while at home, has a social life quite different to that of free-ranging domestic dogs. What are we humans to our dogs? Simply access to resources, or is there something more to the relationship? Would they still love us if we stopped feeding, playing with and providing for them? If only they could tell us! As always, though, their behaviour can give us hints, and behavioural science has some insights as well.

We have already introduced the concept of humans as a secure base from which dogs can explore. It is a useful way to think about our relationship with the dogs in our care. We are attachment figures — perhaps like parents, or surrogate parents. Studies suggest that dogs might be even more intensely attached to their owners than human infants are to their parents. Indeed, functional magnetic resonance imaging (fMRI) studies have shown that dogs find the very appearance of their owners to be rewarding. We like to think that our dogs love us, not just because we feed, play with and take care of them, but because we have a relationship that is more meaningful than mere transient rewards. Cheesecake is an excellent item to spend time with, provided you have a spoon, but we don't miss the cheesecake when we're away from it in the same way we miss our loved ones. It is difficult to ask our dogs if they miss us, but we can look at how much time they choose to spend near us if the opportunity is there (try substituting 'dog' for 'cheesecake' in the following questions if you are now unsure about your relationship with cheesecake). How often is your dog in the same room as you? How often does she sleep within arm's length of you? Will she get up from napping so she can follow you to another room? Where would she sleep overnight if she could choose anywhere? Does she return to you if she is startled or threatened? Pay attention to your dog's preferences for proximity to you when you've been home most of the day compared to when you've been out most of the day. Is there a difference? Melissa's dogs generally prefer to be closer to her when she's been out for a few hours than they do when she's been nearby and available for a few hours. This suggests that Melissa is more than just a source of resources. Perhaps she is a resource herself.

Stealing your seat

It is not uncommon to hear of dogs who somehow magically appear on your spot on the sofa within moments of your leaving it. Do they want what's yours? Are they trying to inconvenience you? Are they showing you they are dominant? The answer is probably much simpler: your buttocks left the spot warm and smelling like you. Plus, if you happen to spend a lot of time in that spot, it is associated with you temporally (in time) and spatially (in space). So, in one sense, it's a mighty fine place to wait for your return. Perhaps, in addition, your dog is drawn

We are much more than just dog owners to our dogs.

to items that other members of the social group have recently spent time with, just in case they're valuable. You can always test the motivation behind this habit. What does your dog do if you play with an item for a while and then put it down? A dog drawn to an item that is of interest to other members of the group might investigate or even pick it up. We add value to articles by playing with them, and simply by holding and possessing them. What if you left a heat pack under a clean towel, next to a recently worn (but not warm) item of your clothing? Which one is most attractive to your dog? If she's not interested in either, try sitting between them (or on both of them) for a minute and then get up. So, studying the behaviour of the dog reveals its preference. Science!

Humans as super-leaders?

We have already discussed what dogs like, and that includes company, whether that is familiar humans or familiar dogs. Dogs who do not have human families and are allowed to associate with whomever they wish, tend to adopt a social strategy based on how plentiful resources are and how they are distributed. Scarce food that is distributed throughout the area creates ongoing competition as the dogs scavenge for it, and tolerance of competitors is stretched if there is not enough food to support a group of dogs. This is most often the case in human settlements where dogs roam free, and dogs are usually living on their own or with one other dog. Food that is more readily available or is concentrated in small areas might create a different dynamic — dogs might find that banding together is more beneficial and sustainable. In these cases, dogs seem to devote time to grooming and positively interacting with each other, which likely helps to bind the group. Some dogs in a group also develop a preference to be close to particular members of the group, which extends to following that member wherever they go, showing us that in the dog world leaders are created by the behaviour of their followers, who stick close to them by choice, not by their ability to directly influence those around them. So, if dog owners are attachment figures for their dogs, what does that really mean? Are dog owners also leaders?

Social dominance in dogs — the alpha of the pack?

It would be remiss of us not to address the elephant in the room at this point; namely, dominance in dogs. It is a prevalent belief that domestic dogs struggle to be the so-called 'alpha of the pack', and that it is important for humans to disabuse our dogs of this notion. This has led to inhumane practices centred around forcing a dog to submit to humans, punitive actions for perceived attempts to ascend the pecking order, and a whole lot of fanciful mythology on how to be the alpha. The current scientific literature on social dominance in dogs acknowledges that it may often exist between dogs. Whether this includes humans or not has not been examined.

There are a few key points to remember about social dominance that may help you make sense of what you hear. It is about priority access to resources. Dominant animals tend to get the resources they want when they want them. Humans nearly always have this by default.

The best predictor of a dominant animal is that other individuals defer to him. This means the dominant animal is granted access to resources by other members of the group, rather than taking them by force. Don't bother trying to MAKE your dog submit to you. Likely you will just scare the poor dog.

Dogs are socially flexible! Every group might adopt a slightly different pathway to social harmony. Some groups can manage this with a lot of negotiation and sharing, while others might be more despotic. We humans are unlikely to be included in this: we do not

typically compete with our dogs and lack the mobility of body parts to let us signal with the subtlety required in doggy conversations.

Social organisation is fascinating, but not important in making your dog happy. It is not necessary in training or management of your dog. Your role as primary caregiver is to manage — if dogs in your house are having regular, tense conversations about resource access, your role is to ease the competition and tension as much as possible. Dogs are not good sharers and it's best not to expect them to share, or they will have to rely heavily on their negotiation skills. They are brilliantly flexible, but not endlessly so!

The Special One

In most households, at least one human will be the primary caregiver for the resident dog. That person will feed the dog, open doors or gates for him, play with him, take him for walks and train him. Human caregivers can perhaps be considered super-leaders from the perspective of many domestic dogs. Humans have access to nearly all the resources that matter and they have control over the dog's own home environment as well. What's more, they are the ones who allow him access to those resources, who provide safety in the face of potential threats and who spend time playing with him and stroking his ears (while free-ranging dogs often affectionately nuzzle each other). In contrast to other dogs, these super-leaders can make the Magic Car-thing open its doors and even move, they can scratch those hard-to-reach places at the front of a dog's chest, and they can even remove skin and paw irritants, such as thorns. What better individual to stick close to? Such a human might appear very attractive to dogs living in a social group, prompting dogs to follow them from room to

Dogs like to spend time in close proximity to their favourite human.

room, just as they would follow their preferred group member as they moved around the territory in a free-living state. Near that special member of the group is definitely the best place for a dog to sleep if he wants to ensure he is never far from the action, so it is unsurprising that dogs allowed to sleep wherever they like in a household often choose the bedroom (even better, the bed) of their special person or people.

To be alone is tolerable; to be separated is torture

Research on free-ranging dogs shows that dogs can live on their own but, if they lived in a group, under what circumstances would they choose to be away from their group? When and why would they choose not to accompany their favourite member of their group, if that member left the area? Remember, in the free-ranging state, there is no such thing as a door or a wall, a gate or a fence. So, not following a favourite group member is not an outcome imposed by physical barriers as it is in the domestic setting. Choosing not to follow a favourite group member would likely require some deeply conflicting goals, such as nursing pups, avoiding pain or ongoing conflict with another member of the group, or avoiding perceived danger in a new environment. Is it any surprise our dogs nearly always wish to accompany us when we leave the house? The allure of an adventure with The Most Reliable Source of Good Stuff is sure to contribute to the distress domestic dogs commonly show when they are left behind. That said, it does not account for all that distress.

To be alone is a state that domestic dogs can evidently tolerate, but to be separated from their group is a different state all together. To be

Many dogs would choose to sleep on the bed with their favourite human than on their own bed.

separated is to be cast adrift and without the support that makes group-living the preferred strategy in that environment. To be separated is to possibly miss out on access to resources that the group obtains together. Our dogs can certainly learn to tolerate being left alone by their human family, but they could be inherently unprepared for this eventuality. What is a dog separated from her group to do?

In the best possible scenario, she might perhaps take advantage of being alone by exploring and maybe finding resources she will have the luxury of not having to defend from other group members. Some serial yard-escapists could be doing just this. If fruitful exploration is not an option, though, or if the dog is not the type to explore on her own, there is not much for her to do but wait for her group to return. This may be particularly worrisome for dogs who have been left in novel surroundings (for example: a house that is not theirs, or a vet clinic or a boarding facility) or for dogs who do not live with other companion animals and/or with only one human. In these cases, perhaps being separated is more intense an experience than when only one member of a larger group is away.

This is especially valuable to keep in mind when bringing a new dog into the household, particularly a rescue dog who might have recently spent time in a kennel situation where life may have been very stressful. Some dogs cope phenomenally well with transition into a new home, but it is worth remembering that we can't tell a dog that this now is their home. We can't reassure them that separation from their group is temporary. To them, they are in an unfamiliar place and the one who feeds them has abandoned them. The uncertainty could be formidable. And, if chewing stuff or barking lessens the pain, these responses become the default coping mechanisms. It may be worth

It is not a natural state for dogs to be separated from their human family.

taking the time to gently prepare a new dog for being left alone before it needs to be done for extended periods. Short outings starting at less than a minute and building up to longer periods can assist a dog in understanding that they will not be permanently abandoned.

Attachment: the good, the bad and the ugly

Dog owners who report signs of strong attachment from their dog generally tend to report their relationship with their dog is highly positive and satisfying. It is likely that human–dog relationships are largely built on humans provisioning dogs with food. Dogs need the food that humans make available and most humans enjoy feeding their dogs. But beyond meeting this basic need, providing play and positive physical contact and being aware of and responsive to the emotional state of the dog are mutually satisfying to both parties. Spending quality time with your dogs where you are interacting with them, seeing them in a variety of contexts and around novel stimuli, working towards training goals, playing, discovering what they enjoy and how they show it puts you in the perfect place to develop a healthy attachment bond with your dogs. All of this interaction creates a two-way street, although the characteristics of the resulting bond in either direction often differ. A healthy attachment is one that allows you both to enjoy being around each other, enjoy interacting with each other, and building a mountain of positive outcomes for both of you. This comes easily when you know your dog. It is easy to see the state dogs are in and respond with empathy, as you would with a friend or child. When your dog interacts fully with you, he will most likely respond to your care favourably, meaning he is amenable to cooperating with you. The result is a relationship with your canine pal in which you are both sensitive to each other, and the sense of two-way communication is very real.

Scientists are still seeking to understand attachment styles between dogs and their owners. Attachment between human children and their parents, and between human adults, is not always wholly positive. Sometimes one or both individuals becomes very clingy, seeming to need their attachment figure to feel safe. We see some dogs that are dependent on their owners and will not willingly leave the safe haven their owner represents. This may be associated with chronic anxiety in dogs, which can manifest as extreme distress when owners prepare to leave their dog in the home, and warrants seeking professional assistance. Remember that attachment can change throughout a dog's or human's life. An increase in a dog's distress at being left, or unusually intense and prolonged excitement upon reuniting, may be worth discussing in a professional consultation.

Another attachment style in humans is labelled anxious-avoidant and is characterised by independence and seemingly resisting connecting with their attachment figure at all. Attachment avoidance is more a characteristic of some humans' bonds with their dogs than vice versa, possibly to avoid the anticipated sadness of parting as occurs during grief. It seems unlikely that dogs can be so emotionally complicated, but we do see owners who need more connection with their dog than the dog really wants to offer. What can result is a needy human, trying to push themselves on a dog, with physical contact and perhaps hand feeding, often trying to prompt the dog to come to them. Meanwhile, the dog could take or leave these interactions and may become increasingly difficult to engage as he anticipates interactions that are not terribly positive for him. If you find you are often approaching your dog to try to get him to pay attention to you, either so you can keep him safe or interact with him, stop and think how you can turn this around. Understanding how he has bonded to you can help you to work with him and providing the traits of good attachment (security, responsiveness to him, positive outcomes) can encourage him to seek you out.

The third attachment style known in human infants is anxious-ambivalent. This is characterised by anxiety when an attachment figure is absent, yet apparent reluctance to approach the figure when they return. This is thought to be a factor of inconsistent caregiving, with the attachment figure sometimes responding to the infant positively and sometimes negatively. Sadly, it is not difficult to create this pattern in a dog if the human attachment figure is also prone to rebuffing or even making aggressive outbursts towards the dog. You could know dogs that seem to adore their owners despite their owners sometimes shouting at them, throwing things at them, or even striking them. Why does the dog still approach in a friendly manner? Why does the dog apparently want to be close to this owner? We don't know for sure but there might be a variety of plausible reasons. It's possible the dog is attached socially to this person because of their role in providing food and probably, at times, positive contact.

Research has shown that unpleasant outcomes become most stressful when an animal cannot predict or avoid them. An attachment figure who sometimes behaves threateningly but, at other times, provides very positive outcomes could create the exact situation in which an animal is most helpless and distressed by the conflict of never knowing when to stay away and when to approach.

A healthy attachment with your dog allows you both to enjoy being together.

9

CARING FOR YOUR DOG FROM PUPPY TO OLD AGE

**T**HE PUPPY YOU BRING HOME AT EIGHT WEEKS OLD WILL CHANGE DRAMATICALLY IN HER FIRST YEAR.

And she will continue to do so in her second year. After that, the changes might slow down, but she will keep changing as she grows older, just as humans do. Humans don't do all the developing we are ever going to do, both physically and mentally, by the time we reach sexual maturity. (Fortunately, adolescence isn't our developmental end-point, or vampire-related romance novels might be the height of human literary accomplishment.)

This chapter will lead you through dog development and how a dog's needs might change as they grow older. Puppyhood, adolescence and early adulthood are perhaps the phases in which our dogs need the most attention and input from us, but their senior years are when they need most love and compassion, and we owe them that after all the years of companionship they have given.

Baby dogs

We discussed the socialisation window in Chapter 8, but it is important to remember that dogs are still accumulating history with stimuli they encounter after that socialisation period has ended. Ensuring your baby dog builds the history that will be most desirable to you and him when he is a young dog is more easily achieved if we appreciate a few features that set puppies apart from adult dogs.

Your puppy has a lot to learn as he grows into an adult dog.

Puppies are hard-wired to approach social objects and befriend them. Many, but not all, puppies are like little heat-seeking missiles that close in on their target. On making contact, the average puppy will then try to tell his target that he is a baby and may need provisioning and/or playful interactions. He does this by wagging his tail low and furiously, while trying to lick a mouth — any mouth. Paws also often become involved in this endeavour. An adult dog's response to this barrage may be to sniff the puppy's genitals to collect information on who he is. The puppy often rolls over onto his back to facilitate this, and possibly to remind the adult dog that puppies are definitely, absolutely, no threat. It is a vulnerable position for a puppy to be in, as he can't really get up without possibly offending the adult dog until the adult dog backs off to make room.

Puppies can quickly go from delighted to terrified if an unusual stimulus or lack of autonomy worries them. It is therefore good practice to keep monitoring to check if he is enjoying a given interaction by giving him a clear opportunity to end it. Step back, give him space to move, encourage him to come away from that other dog or person and return to you, the secure base. Let him make his own decision on whether to go back to the encounter for more mouth-licking, pawing and tail-wagging,

Not all pups engage this way. Some are rather shy wallflowers, or they can become easily overwhelmed and start barking. Equally, they can react strongly to certain arousing stimuli, such as running children, skateboards or moving cars, by barking or lunging. It might be cute when your puppy tries to fiercely chase a car, but it's not a safe habit to get into. In all of these cases, creating space, encouraging the puppy to stay calm with gentle stroking, soothing words and a quiet

Puppies tend to solicit social interactions with fierce abandon.

tone can go a long way towards helping him develop a sensible emotional response to objects in our shared world.

Puppies have a particular need to be close to their family. A puppy is at the prime time of her life to develop a healthy attachment to the humans and other companion animals in her family. She is still far from being an independent adult, so she will naturally tend to see you — the one who feeds and interacts with her — as a source of safety and security. This is most necessary for pups because they have a lot to learn about the world. They need you to look out for them and make sure they don't get themselves in serious trouble, such as becoming trapped in a space that used to accommodate them when they were smaller or endangered by approaching an adult dog who is not puppy-tolerant. Take advantage of this tendency to want to be close, by training the puppy to find you when you call him and, of course, come when you call him, to walk on a loose leash, and reward him for attending to you. He may be particularly good at what's known as social referencing — reading the expressions of others and using the information to help make decisions. If he becomes afraid of a novel item or stimulus, you can give him neutral or positive emotional signals about that stimulus, and perhaps approach it and interact confidently and playfully with it. If you're a convincing actor, you'll soon notice how emboldening these signals are for him.

The downside of this engagement with us and attachment to us as care-givers is that puppies are particularly distressed at being left alone. It's possible they have never been left alone before if their mother was not given space to leave them for lengthening periods as they approached weaning. This is an area of canine science that begs for closer scrutiny. There are many suggestions for how to manage a

Puppies typically become highly distressed if they are separated from the family.

puppy's distress at being left alone. Some advocate taking no time off work to welcome the puppy into the household, expecting him to master being left alone immediately and with no assistance. In contrast, we suggest that time devoted to a puppy's socialisation is always well spent, but that doesn't mean imposing ourselves on the pup 24 hours a day.

Think about the early days in a new home from the puppy's perspective. She has been taken from her mother and siblings, with whom she has been all her life. She is in an unfamiliar place with unfamiliar smells, unfamiliar people and maybe other unfamiliar animals. She is still dependent, but the one who feeds and cares for her disappears with little warning and sometimes for long periods. In the case of feral dogs, the pups have each other for company when the dam leaves the den to forage. Not so for the domestic pups. What are they to do with themselves? Vocalise themselves to the point of fatigue? Far too many do and others just happen to be whining when the care-giver returns, learning a persistent lesson that vocalising is always worth a try. Instead of demanding that pups tolerate these abrupt and lengthy departures, it seems kinder to take the time to slowly introduce them to both life with you, and being left alone. They may adjust quickly to both if they come to expect that you are probably nearby if they need you. Taking time off work for this sort of training also helps you house-train the puppy if, for example, you are aware of when they have just woken up. You can slowly increase the time they are aware of you not being in sight, and help them accept your absence by leaving them with toys to play with, items to chew or food puzzle toys to work on.

The two-speed puppy: warp speed and dead to the world

Puppies are like any juvenile animal: they sleep more than adults, and often so soundly that you can sneakily set them up for fun photos with your collection of action figures! Awake, they can be mini-tornadoes of non-stop action, furiously exploring a world in which just about everything is new and exciting and either edible or fun to play with, or both. If they cannot be supervised, they should be contained safely so that they don't tornado your favourite items into tiny pieces. It is possible to contain a puppy tornado inside a puppy pen, crate or run. Give the pup items that he is allowed to destroy: it is the puppy way. Most puppies are very easily distracted because the world is an explosion of novelty for them and they are yet to develop an attention span. Work to their strengths by training in short bursts of only a few minutes, with lots of play and lots of treats to keep their attention for longer than it takes to sneeze.

Puppies don't stay puppies for long, so it's best to embrace their nature, let their enthusiasm for the world infect you and accept that they are immature and there is plenty of time for them to become the perfect dog you envision. Work on being their safe haven to retreat to, their secure base to explore from, and a source of many pleasant and exciting resources and reinforcers. Concentrate on giving them opportunities to become familiar with the world, but always at their own pace.

Your dog's an adolescent now ... So sorry!

Puppies grow up all too soon. They become lanky and, at times, display some baffling proportions as they grow into their bodies from about 6 months to 12–18 months old. At some stage during this period, or for all of this period if you're really unlucky, your beautiful, sweet puppy

will become a horror. This is the time of a dog's life when he is ready for some independence and to live large. In adolescence, dogs often become extremely active and there will be that day when you call him and, instead of whirling on a pinhead to leap into your arms, he will gallop in the opposite direction to make a nuisance of himself with other dogs or children. He may well embarrass you and will act as if he's never been trained in his life. He will be teething for at least some of this time, and thus feel the need to chomp his way beaver-like through your house and belongings. That cute puppy tornado whirling through life is now a category 5 storm, leaving you wondering where you went wrong.

DON'T PANIC. Adolescent dogs are a handful and that's why, sadly, this seems to be the most common age for dogs to be surrendered to shelters for problematic behaviour. It's typical for dogs of this age to be a little nightmarish. Hang in there: his brain will grow back sooner or later! In the meantime, accept that, just like the teenage human, he is (probably) not actively trying to vex you, and this is not how he will be for the rest of his life. You might even find he is different from day to day: sometimes an angel; other days a big, fat embarrassment. Manage the dog you woke up to today with the goal of ensuring he doesn't get to practise behaviour you don't want him to do. This could mean he has to go back on a long leash for a while until he reliably comes when called again. You might have to work hard on ensuring he doesn't pull while on the leash. You could find he is suddenly barking and lunging at stimuli that never bothered him before, or reacting to every single unusual sight or sound encountered at home.

As they go through this awkward phase, dogs are simply finding their place in the world and they need your patience and guidance,

Puppies play hard and sleep hard.

even if they seem to think they know what they're doing. Help them make good decisions by throwing out suggestions (for example: 'Come and sit with me, rather than declaring war on the postman') and rewarding if they follow them. If you do not want her waging war on the postman, make sure you have taken appropriate precautions for her ignoring your suggestion or your possible misjudgment of how responsive she might be under certain circumstances. Barriers and restraints are a great way to ensure dogs can't practise unwanted behaviour. While offering her alternative responses and managing her ability to practise unwelcome behaviours, you should keep being her attachment figure and building your relationship. Remember that your dog still has a lot to learn, especially about 'talking dog' with other dogs. Positive interactions with dogs of different sizes and ages can help canine adolescents learn good dog manners with all kinds of conspecifics (the scientific word for 'other individuals of the same species'). That said, dogs of this age are most likely to overstep social boundaries and earn themselves a disciplinary snap, especially if they don't adjust their behaviour in response to other dogs. In particular, small or older dogs may not be interested in boisterous wrestling but, regardless of this, the adolescent dog might try to provoke them into playing anyway.

Adolescent dogs might be prone to making decisions without your input, but they have to earn their freedom to act on these decisions. Your job is to assess the risk of these decisions getting them hurt, hurting or frightening others, or practising unwanted behaviour, and this includes with other dogs. All dogs seem to make better decisions and be more responsive to others when they are less aroused, so you can help out your canine adolescents by interrupting play frequently and practising a few tricks (preferably trained behaviours that demand a modicum of calmness) before letting them go back to play. If they are too often allowed to make social mistakes, they could learn that other dogs aren't much fun. You are helping them, as well as other dogs and their owners, by ensuring they don't provoke aggression from other dogs. Dogs in this age group might benefit from being kept busy at home with lots of enrichment activities and physical exercise. However, repetitive activities such as pounding the pavement to the point of exhaustion can damage joints and so should be avoided until dogs are fully grown.

Maturity, blessed maturity

One day, you will wake up and discover your adolescent category 5 storm appears to have been downgraded. She will suddenly become more responsive to you, and she might even be able to endure a day of only negligible exercise without developing cabin fever and bouncing off the walls. You might find she is less likely to bark and considerably less desperate to chew everything in sight. Congratulations! Your dog is just about a grown-up and is showing hints of the sweet, biddable canine soul you hoped for. Hopefully, she has experienced many stimuli and learned to accept them as normal, setting her up for making default assessments about future novel encounters as largely unremarkable. You might find that, if necessary, you can reduce her exercise and enrichment activities without unwelcome consequences, such as chewing of your dining-room chair legs. Nonetheless, we know that those who play together stay together, so it is worthwhile continuing to spend quality time with your dog, playing, offering rewards for good behaviours, and being there to provide safety and security when needed.

As they reach social maturity, many dogs switch strategies when meeting unfamiliar dogs and people. While as puppies and adolescents they would rush to interact with every object, social maturity will see them, in many cases, shift to a casual sniff, circle and move on. They may continue to play with familiar dogs, and might find compatible playmates in unfamiliar dogs, but they often lose that beguiling youthful motivation to forge playful interactions with all kinds of dogs. It is important to monitor carefully as they make this transition into adulthood, as their preferences may change. Their tolerance for interactions that don't entirely suit them can decline as well. They might also become more assertive when they are adopting distance-increasing behaviours.

Enrichment is for all life stages

We have mentioned enrichment several times in this book, but what exactly is it? Enrichment is the introduction of stimuli that encourage mental and physical engagement in natural activities and can be considered under two broad banners: behavioural and environmental. Natural activities for dogs include, but are not limited to, tracking scents, chasing moving objects, foraging for food, chewing, tugging, digging, extracting food from containers, finding edible items among non-edible items, problem-solving, exploring, breed-related activities (such as herding for herding dogs) and social interactions. There are endless ways to add enrichments to your dog's daily life, limited only by your imagination.

Most dogs enjoy working on commercially available or home-made puzzle toys that release food slowly depending on how the dogs manipulate the device. For more energetically costly forms of enrichment, digging, swimming and playing tug or retrieve are good choices for dogs with a lot of energy to burn. These can all be made more challenging by incorporating mental tasks; for example, can you get your dog to dig in the exact spot you indicate? Can you combine swimming and retrieving, or reward tricks with a retrieve? Of course, not all dogs are equally blessed with problem-solving and manipulative skills, so enrichment activities should be made easier or more difficult depending on the skills of the dog in question. Paul's dogs exalt in the opportunity to swim, especially with humans. Melissa's dogs all seem to regard hikes in the bush as the ultimate form of enrichment. The rough terrain requires constant mental processing to navigate successfully and the environment is brimming with interesting scents. Trick training is another favourite, but any form of training is probably just as enriching as long as it is based on earning rewards.

Senior dogs and golden oldies

Research we have conducted in our own lab suggests that dogs become less bold and sociable as they get older. They are less likely to approach unfamiliar dogs and people, less likely to play with these strangers and less likely to approach novel objects. Perhaps there is a 'been there, done that' aspect to their lifetime experience that means they naturally become less interested in activities they have done many times before, but there is probably more to it than that. We have known dogs who have enjoyed playing fetch, for example, well into their senior years and this preference for favoured forms of fun appears far more persistent and less variable than a love of social interactions. Perhaps that variability is the real key to a decline in sociability and boldness. Dogs have positive, neutral and negative outcomes to encounters with novel items and social interactions with strangers. It could be that, over time, the negative interactions begin to erode dogs' willingness to take on risks with strangers and novel objects. They may become more pessimistic.

It is also possible that dogs become less behaviourally flexible as they grow older, just as humans do. This can manifest in decreasing tolerance of variable outcomes, such as social interactions and

investigating novelty. Perhaps mature dogs also become more habitual individuals, so that they increasingly rely on favoured behavioural strategies that have been most effective in the past. Interestingly, rather than affecting puppies and adolescents, noise phobias (such as fear of thunder and fireworks) commonly appears in adult dogs of three years and over. This indicates that mature dogs are less welcoming of change than their youthful counterparts.

In short, it pays to think carefully before expecting mature dogs to tolerate a steady stream of strangers and novel stimuli, and perhaps even familiar but unusually intense stimuli, as well as they did when younger. Be alert for signs of conflict or avoidance. Adding a new dog to the household when the resident dog is a senior is a common strategy, but should be approached carefully, with the means to separate both dogs. This will allow you to give the senior dog a break from the new dog at times, and keep them both safe when you are not supervising them.

Dogs also become more prone to pain and disease as they get older. Pain can be difficult to detect. Think of how stiff or sore you need to be before it affects how you move. You can appear perfectly functional while experiencing significant pain. Dogs tend to be stoic, and by the time they are limping, grumbling or yelping, or are unusually disinterested in their favourite activities, they are probably suffering a lot. How do we detect subtle signs of pain that could be associated with injury or illness? Perhaps we need to note that a dog who is uncomfortable becomes irritable, growling or snapping at other dogs or members of the family over minor transgressions that would normally be tolerated. Dogs have bad days, one assumes, but it always pays to look for patterns. That's why our small army of dogloggers like

Dogs may change their enjoyment of particular activities as they mature.

doglogbook. When it holds enough data on your dog, the *doglogbook* website reveals these patterns. Does he often have a bad day after a run at the beach? Are his levels of activity declining? A dog who has periods of restlessness, pacing or becoming more prone to alert barking might be experiencing pain or discomfort somewhere in his body, or even hunger. These signs may come and go, or be associated with his usual daily activities, such as eating meals. Consult a veterinarian any time there is an inexplicable change in your dog's behaviour, and maintain regular health checks.

Dogs are considered seniors at eight years and older. Dogs of this age may develop a series of conditions, but one that is especially worthy of discussion is canine cognitive decline, or doggy dementia. As with some humans, approximately 15 per cent of older dogs can start to show disruptions in how they respond to stimuli. Early signs include pacing in circles, appearing confused at times and being unable to find the source of enticing scents, such as a treat on the floor. Other symptoms of this condition may include loss of house-training, disrupted sleep cycles so that they wake repeatedly during the night, becoming lost in familiar surroundings, going to the wrong side of a doorway (trying to get through the hinged side, rather than the open side) and seemingly forgetting their name. It can make dogs challenging to care for when their behaviour can become aggravating or disruptive to the household. Research has shown that training throughout a dog's life, focusing on problem-solving and attention, can help ward off canine cognitive decline. Even without a cognitive deficit, older dogs may lose their sight, their hearing, they may find movement increasingly painful, eating difficult if they have dental disease, and they can become grumpy. Nevertheless, while our old dogs

Senior dogs require extra care and monitoring.
We owe it to them.

may no longer be the canine pal full of joy and vitality that we have enjoyed for so many years, they can still live a quality life, and we owe that to them as their carers. It may be necessary to reduce their physical activity and be mindful that they are more frail than they used to be. So, sharp changes in direction, running and traversing rough terrain or even walks on smooth terrain may become painful for them. This does not necessarily mean they would be happiest as a homebody. If they can comfortably get in the car (perhaps with a ramp or the help of a sling for lifting), they can go for drives for a change of scenery or to meet old friends. They can even get out for a short explore. Your job as the carer of your old canine friend is what it has always been. Be a source of reinforcers, safety and security. Make life easier for them wherever and however you can. Find ways to help them engage in the activities they have always loved most and enjoy them together.

The final goodbye

No one wants to think about their dog leaving them forever, but end-of-life decisions are among the most important we make for our dogs and their happiness. There comes a time when there is not very much happiness left in their life. Perhaps they have become too frail for all the activities they used to find joy in? Perhaps essential maintenance activities, such as squatting to defecate, have become painful? Perhaps they are in pain even when resting? Has their life become reduced to lying in one spot, eliminating and eating? Maybe they have conditions that are being treated, but the treatment is becoming less effective or more invasive? People are fond of saying you will know when it's time to say goodbye because your beloved dog will 'tell you'. This is one time that maybe asking the dog is not so helpful and it was precisely why we developed *doglogbook* — to put data behind end-of-life decisions so that veterinarians can advise owners based on each dog's own individual notes.

Physical and mental decline is not a neat journey with a clear point when a dog no longer wants to live. We don't know if dogs can grasp the concept of life and death. They fight to live because that is what life does. After consulting with your veterinarian and, hopefully, sharing your *doglogbook* data, you need to decide when your dog is no longer happy enough for you to continue inflicting life on them. You decide when their suffering from hour-to-hour outweighs the little snippets of joy they still have, and ask: 'Is my dog living a life that is worth living?' How do we measure a life worth living? By the opportunities available for the individual to experience joy, access reinforcers, be enriched. If those opportunities are fast diminishing, it is time to ask that question and keep asking it on a regular basis until the answer is 'no'.

10

CHOOSING A DOG YOU CAN BE HAPPY WITH

# ATTACHMENT IS THE BASIS OF YOUR RELATIONSHIP WITH YOUR DOG.

And attachment is a two-way street. In principle, you could be doing everything appropriate to forge a strong bond with your dog but your relationship may be derailed by frustration on both sides if your dog's temperament or exercise requirements are beyond what you can practically manage. This chapter will delve into the uncertain world of selecting dogs who will, hopefully, match your lifestyle so that you can be happy making them happy. Before we go any further, we should stress that predicting future dog behaviour is a bit like shopping for fresh produce: some features seem evident from just a glance, but we can spend a long time examining our options without really knowing how anything we can detect is likely to relate to the taste. This chapter is a guide at best. We cannot tell you a fool-proof way to get the dog you want.

First, identify what you want

It can be very hard to choose a dog if you like any dog that makes eye contact with you! Try to think beyond beguiling canine expressions and velvety ears to reveal what you want life to look and feel like with your anticipated canine friend. Should the dog be easy to train and get along with? Or are you up for the challenge of a dog who needs reasons to do what you ask; reasons beyond 'because I said so'? Do you want a

Do you want a dog that can't wait to find out what you need, or a dog who can amuse herself?

companion for watching television and easy walks down to the shops? Or are you looking for a running or biking buddy? Do you love lots of physical contact, or do you appreciate your own space more often than not? Will you be at home a lot, or is this dog going to need to be content alone for most of the day while you're at work? How many neighbours do you have and how tolerant are they likely to be of barking? Also consider how much grooming you are willing to do. 'I like brushing dogs' may not prepare you for a dense, long double coat like Kivi's that needs patient detangling on a weekly basis. (A jar of peanut butter, with 'Dogs only' written on it to avoid embarrassing mistakes, can gain willing cooperation with grooming — one minute of brushing buys the dog five seconds with the peanut butter jar!)

Exercise and grooming requirements and training ease are all critical to consider when acquiring a dog, but you might also consider personality and behavioural tendencies. Are there any that would represent problems you'd rather avoid? For example, highly persistent dogs can be great for an experienced trainer or someone who wants to do dog sports, but they can be a trial to live with. Analysing dog personalities can be like critiquing modern art: many traits and dimensions have been suggested, but it's hard to pin down what nature has created. We will focus on the most common and predictive traits.

Dog traits to consider

Activity: Dogs who spend most of their time cantering from one activity to the next are likely to remain energetic throughout their life. Likewise, dogs who walk (or plod) for much of the time are likely to remain low energy. This does not necessarily reflect the dogs' exercise requirements, but has a profound bearing on what these different dogs

Make sure you can meet exercise and grooming requirements before settling on a breed.

are like to live with. It is worthwhile picturing a combination of dog size and activity contained within your house, yard and car. A 50 kg (8 stone) dog that bounds through life can find himself on your kitchen counters without much trouble. (So can a 12 kg/2 stone dog of similar activity levels.) While a 50 kg dog who seems unaware that more than one of his paws can leave the ground simultaneously may actually be well suited to smaller indoor environments.

Resilience: The canine attribute of resilience captures how quickly a dog can recover from a disturbance, such as a startling stimulus or an unusual event. Resilient dogs recover quickly and move on. ('Wow, that was weird! Looks like I'm safe though.') Bundy oozes this trait and routinely and swiftly forgives anyone and everyone for transgressions that reliably stun or dismay other dogs around him. Dogs lacking resilience take longer to establish that they are safe and may be prone to being startled or defending themselves from other unexpected stimuli that are presented soon after. This is called 'trigger stacking' in dog-trainer vernacular and refers to how dogs can react more strongly than usual to stimuli if they have not yet recovered from another recent arousing experience. Such dogs might not be a good fit for a busy household or neighbourhood, but may do fine in quieter environments where life is more peaceful.

Aggression: It is questionable whether aggression should be considered a personality trait at all. Aggression is one strategy dogs can use to meet their goals. Perhaps it would be accurate to say that some dogs are more likely to adopt aggressive responses than others. However, we don't know whether that level of aggression is inherent to their personality or if they happen to experience emotional events more keenly than other dogs. Furthermore, they may simply tend to

Is your home large enough to contain a dog
of this size, energy levels and grooming needs?

opt for a proactive coping style more often than a reactive or passive coping style. We will discuss these coping styles in a little more detail later in this chapter. Aggression is uncommon in puppies, so if you are viewing a puppy who is using aggression, not just with other littermates but with humans and adult dogs, you would do well to think carefully how you might manage this behaviour if it persists as the dog grows.

Impulsivity: This is an interesting personality trait that is currently attracting research attention. Impulsivity in dogs is thought to have three components: behavioural regulation; responsiveness; and aggression and response to novelty. Impulsive dogs are the impatient souls of the dog world and do not seem to plan much before simply launching into action. They may become highly aroused and excited over relatively low-key events. Impulsive dogs can also be persistent in pursuing their goals and prone to aggression if they become frustrated or excited. Typically, they are not easy to train and could not really be considered emotionally steady. They may rapidly swing between emotional highs and lows, which probably reflects how readily they become aroused. Impulsive dogs much prefer immediate positive outcomes to having to wait a short while for an even better outcome. They want it and they want it now!

Impulsive dogs certainly have their charm if you are the kind of person who likes exciting, dynamic training or play sessions and witnessing canine creativity at its most startling. They are great fun for people who enjoy dogs who apply an impetuous energy persistently and excitedly to attain their goals. (Note that dog goals may or may not be compatible with human values.) Impulsive dogs should come with a warning sticker: 'Recommended for dog enthusiasts only.' If you do find yourself with a dog who seizes the day in her jaws and can be described with words like 'livewire' and 'firecracker' and 'unpredictable', it may be comforting to know that, with the right help, dogs can learn to control their impulses. Establishing a *sit to ask nicely* rule is a good place to start.

Coping styles (proactive/active vs reactive/passive): Coping styles are a topic of interest in laboratory rodent research. There may be some overlap between coping styles and impulsivity. A dog can be a proactive (or active) coper, which means he actively tries to solve problems. This might manifest as tackling problems head-on (for example, rushing and barking), or running in the opposite direction. Research suggests that these proactive copers may also be routine-driven and decide quickly, based on very few signals, which activity they should be doing. They may also be more prone to aggression.

In contrast, a reactive (or passive) coping style characterises dogs who are more likely to simply freeze or become inactive when faced with a threat. These dogs tend to adopt coping responses that involve quiet avoidance, or they wait uncomfortably until either the threat passes or it becomes evident they have no choice but to act to avoid it. They are labelled 'reactive' because they are more responsive to flux in the environment than proactive individuals and can be easily disturbed by small changes in their surroundings.

Dogs with a proactive coping style might be over-represented in the sub-population of dogs with behaviour problems. However, it's entirely possible that proactive dogs merely show their distress far more obviously and in less acceptable ways than reactive dogs. Consider the dogs who charge around the house barking, howling and destroying property because they have been left alone and contrast them with dogs who seem to withdraw into themselves, making little noise and hardly moving. It is tempting to think that the dogs who make no apparent fuss are coping better than the stress-heads, but the truth is that they may be quietly suffering all the same. Indeed, these dogs could represent an invisible sub-population of dogs who have anxieties or phobias that go undetected and therefore untreated. It can be challenging to manage dogs who have a proactive coping style because they are liable to charge at stimuli they find threatening. Parents with small children who have just been rushed at are unlikely to be pacified by the 'Sorry, my dog has a proactive coping style' line. Proactive dogs can learn to override their urges if they are reinforced lavishly and consistently for preferred behaviours (such as, sit and look at their human) BEFORE they react. Interrupting your dog before they perform an unwanted behaviour is always preferable to trying to train them to choose a different behaviour after they have already performed the unwanted one.

Dogs with a reactive coping style may be comparatively easy to manage compared to their proactive counterparts, but their distress is more difficult to detect. They can be subtle in expressing it, and might not attempt to move away from situations that disturb them until they are extremely uncomfortable or threatened. Kivi defaults to a reactive coping style and his signals of discomfort are easy to miss. Sometimes the most overt sign he offers is the slight averting of his gaze from whatever is bothering him. If he looks away several times, Melissa moves him away to a quieter location to ensure his distress is minimised. Distance gives him the luxury to view the situation from a safer position and allows him to decide if he wants to approach again or stay clear. By observing Kivi's response when a few steps away from the action, Melissa can tell where he wants to be.

Shyness and boldness: The shy–bold continuum has been studied in many species, and is generally used to describe the willingness of an individual to explore novel objects, environments, or other

*Dogs with a proactive coping style rush in to engage
threats, while dogs with a reactive coping style wait it out.*

conspecifics. Bold dogs represent the more resilient and sociable individuals who are less prone to fearfulness than their shy counterparts. Such dogs may be particularly well suited to busy life in cities or suburbia and households with children. Indeed, our research has shown that some of the boldest dog breeds (Staffordshire bull terriers; Labrador retrievers) are also some of the most popular breeds. That said, shyer dogs are not necessarily to be avoided. Perhaps you don't want or need a dog that is the life of the party, but would enjoy a quieter companion who prefers to stick close to the family and avoid potential trouble? Interestingly, research has shown that fearfulness is the least consistent personality trait in dogs. The timid puppy of the litter, who seems prone to cowering, is not necessarily going to grow into a timid, fearful adult dog. Kivi is a perfect example of a shy puppy who grew into a highly sociable, confident, easy-going adult dog.

Trainability: It's no secret that some dogs seem terribly interested in working with humans while others are deeply disinterested in what their human pals might want of them. As a general rule, breeds that were developed to work closely with humans and take direction from them, such as those in the herding and gundog groups, tend to be especially amenable to adopting our human goals as their own. This tendency is amplified if we provide a little incentive in the form of reinforcement. For some dogs, that reinforcement can be as little as a 'Good dog!' from a human; others might require a more tangible reward, such as food or toys. Hounds, northern breeds (Siberian huskies, Samoyeds), Molosser breeds (bulldogs, mastiffs) and livestock guardian breeds have traditionally required less human input and are more likely to get on with business on their own.

There is certainly variation in trainability within breeds, but picking a breed not known for its ease of training may set you up for considerable frustration. This frustration is magnified if you are not prepared to be largely irrelevant to your dog until he wants something. Breeds considered difficult to train are often intelligent and, like any dog, will behave in ways that benefit them. However, they are likely motivated by goals that do not involve humans. Remember Kestrel's keen interest in rapid exploration? The activity she is most motivated to perform does not necessarily include her humans. Likewise, scent-hounds and sight-hounds zoom in on stimuli they have been bred to focus on (olfactory and visual stimuli, respectively) and follow them relentlessly. Praise probably doesn't mean much to them, and nor does a stern tone. This can be infuriating and baffling to people who are accustomed to dogs who dance for joy when a human smiles at them or melt if spoken to firmly. These dogs low in trainability are perfectly trainable. We just need to learn what the dog does find meaningful (see Chapter 2) and use that to reinforce desired behaviour.

HUNDS, HOUNDS AND HERDERS: THE TRAINABILITY CONTINUUM

Melissa favours dogs with a streak of independence who are not traditionally easy to train. Kivi and Erik (the hunds) are both spitz breeds (Finnish lapphund and Swedish vallhund). Melissa says you don't get a spitz breed unless you like surprises and have a good sense of humour. Surprises like 'Surprise! I am not recalling today. Instead, I am running into a swamp to plaster foul-smelling mud all through my luxuriously thick coat.' Kivi and Erik are also herding breeds, which are better known for trainability than the northern spitz breeds. Erik is more herder than spitz and shows this in his eagerness to work with Melissa on whatever she might be doing. Kivi, on the other hand, is more spitz than herder and his cooperation requires plenty of ongoing reinforcement in the form of food. Kestrel's breed is a primitive hound. Despite this shortcoming, she is surprisingly trainable, but she is even more likely than Kivi to abandon her humans in pursuit of her own goals. In these three dogs, trainability can be seen in the motivation level of each dog to interact with their human, how easily they adopt this as their goal when they also have the freedom to explore a novel and exciting environment, and how frequent reinforcement needs to be to maintain their responsiveness to their humans.

Personality combinations

It is important to remember that while the individual traits of a dog might be attractive or unattractive to you, the combination of traits in a given dog can have a dramatic effect on that dog's overall behaviour. Some traits that are mild challenges to manage on their own (such as moderate impulsivity or fearfulness) might become exponentially more difficult to manage when combined with other traits. For example, a dog who is highly active and prone to quick upsurges in arousal might be a bit of a livewire, but if he is easily convinced to change his goals (perhaps because he is also not very persistent or he is very trainable) you have a good chance of being able to channel his behaviour for good. In contrast, when the same traits are combined with low trainability or high aggression (or both) the dog in question may be quick to become aroused, difficult to interrupt, and/or liable to adopt an aggressive strategy when excited. If some shyness or some proneness to fear were also added to the mix, then aggressive reactions are considerably more likely. And if one adds impulsivity, aggressive reactions with little warning are more likely. Go a step further and add low resilience to the combination, then aggressive reactions with little warning are likely to become typical and may promote anxiety. As you can see, several challenging traits in the one dog can snowball into problems that are bigger than the sum of their parts.

Other combinations can reduce the overall impact of one trait. A dog that is highly impulsive but also highly trainable and reasonably resilient is one who is easily aroused, easily rewarded and interested in whatever their human handlers want them to do. This dog is also comfortable in many environments, including many where she might be startled or have a negative experience, such as at dog sports competitions. This is a dog that could be excellent in working roles, such as detection, where the dog may need to work for a long time without reinforcement, or activities such as sports competitions, where reinforcement is not permitted during performance.

It takes practice to recognise personality traits in dogs and predict how they might influence the dog's future behaviour. That said, the predictive power of personality traits may be surprisingly low. Some traits can change over time more than others, and a dog's learning experiences and early environment still have a big influence on their behaviour as an adult. We mentioned that fearfulness is the least consistent personality trait recognised in dogs and it is easy to imagine how a dog's early experiences could profoundly shape how fearful he becomes. We have emphasised several times in this book the importance of experiences: they influence how safe dogs feel in various situations, and how they are likely to respond to stimuli that have previously led to negative experiences. We have also described how repeated positive experiences can encourage optimism and repeated negative experiences can promote pessimism.

It is important to remember that dogs are highly adaptive and can change how they behave to best suit the world that their experiences tell them they live in. Of course, those experiences may not accurately represent the world, and that is why it is so critical to step in on your dog's behalf whenever you see she is uncomfortable or trying to avoid a situation. It is why it is so useful to plan ahead, especially with a puppy or new dog, to do your best to create situations where your dog is most likely to have positive experiences.

Likewise, if you plan to take your dog into a new situation, such as a holiday or a training class, it is a good idea to have a contingency plan for getting them out if they dramatically dislike it. That might include deciding beforehand what behaviour from your dog will prompt you to enact your contingency plan, and where you can take them for an urgent break.

Where to buy your dog or puppy

Our final word on making dogs happy is to address where you will acquire your dog. Early life experiences when the puppy is still with her dam and littermates, and even when she is in her mother's womb, can affect how she develops. Research on laboratory rodents has shown that subjecting a pregnant female to stressful stimuli may result in her young being more emotionally reactive and prone to stress themselves. Likewise, inattentive rodent mothers who do not spend much of their time in physical contact with their young have the same effect: the young grow up prone to strong stress responses, anxiety and emotional reactivity. Laboratory rodents are believed to be a good model for mammals with babies that are helpless without their mother. However, this work has not been repeated in dogs, so it is as yet unknown how a dam's physical health and level of stress while pregnant and caring for her puppies might affect the future behaviour of those puppies.

Have a contingency plan in case it turns out your dog doesn't enjoy a new place or experience.

What does this mean for obtaining a dog? We don't exactly know, but we do know that dogs from commercial puppy breeding facilities ('puppy farms') are more prone to EVERY behaviour problem than dogs from dedicated, boutique breeders. It means that, theoretically, we should consider what environmental conditions a puppy's mother has been in for the past few months before we commit to a puppy from her current litter. Has she been scrounging for enough food to maintain bodyweight? Has she been free of parasites? Has she had a safe denning site where she could give birth and raise her puppies? Was she able to spend time with them but still leave them for short periods? Deprivation of maternal care is damaging, but imposing no escape from the den is also ill advised because it is natural for mothers to leave their young while they forage for food and so on. These maternal absences may help young animals learn to cope with the stress of being separated from their mother, which may in turn protect against separation anxiety and promote stress-coping skills for the future. Scott and Fuller's long-running research programme in the 1960s examined the effects on the development of puppies with low-level stress from short periods of maternal separation in combination with handling and sensory stimulation. It was found that this procedure produced adult dogs who were better at coping with stress, less prone to showing signs of stress, and had better problem-solving skills.

Pedigree or mutt?

Melissa and Paul both have pedigree dogs and have also enjoyed living with mixed-breed dogs. Good dogs abound! So, what is right for you? We don't know, sorry. We're not mind-readers. The advantage of pedigree dogs is that you have the opportunity to meet doggy relatives and gain an appreciation of what behaviour is common. You could get an idea of any health issues in the family. You can also be reasonably confident that a small-scale breeder of pedigree dogs would have kept their bitch in good health and relatively unstressed while she was pregnant and lactating. The disadvantages are that some hereditary diseases are more prevalent in pedigree dogs, and the physical features promoted by breed standards do not always have dog welfare as the highest priority. Breeds with exaggerated features, such as flat faces, very short legs and long backs, may be unusually prone to certain diseases or conditions.

Mixed-breed dogs arguably represent a less predictable option. If the dog's ancestry is unknown, there is less information available on possible health and behaviour outcomes. That said, pedigree dogs do not always act as they are expected to and some apparently did not familiarise themselves with their family tree. Mixed-breed dogs at the first cross may be healthier, or less prone to hereditary diseases, than purebred dogs but evidence of this hybrid vigour is surprisingly difficult to establish. If you don't have specific grand plans for your new dog, you may be just as happy with a mixed-breed as a pedigree. Be aware that mixed-breed dogs are not necessarily free of inherited diseases. Pedigree dog breeders usually ensure they are breeding dogs free of diseases for which health tests are available. Mixed-breed breeders may not take the same care. For further guidance, look up the online RSPCA's *Smart Puppy and Dog Buyer's Guide*.

Adopt and save a life?

There are some terrific dogs who turn up in rescue and dog shelters through no fault of their own. That said, there are also some dogs in shelters with a learning history that might not be ideal. This learning history may lead to very small problem behaviours that are easily overcome, or big behaviour problems. It's often difficult to know until the dog has had a chance to settle into his new home, which may take months. Many rescue centres offer a trial period, so that you can take a dog with a view to adopting, but have the opportunity to check first if it's going to work out with your household and other companion animals. It is okay to send a dog back to a rescue organisation that offered that option, if you do not think you have a good match after all. However, if a trial wasn't offered, or the trial period is over, and you decide the new dog is not a good match, it is your responsibility to make sure the dog finds a home they can be happy in.

Remember that creating a happy dog also depends in part on your being able to be happy with that dog. If you are doubtful the dog will fit in well with you and your lifestyle, there's every chance he will find a home he would be more content in, and you can go on to find a dog you will be better matched with.

Making your dog happy is much easier when they make you happy too. Pick a dog that will match your lifestyle.

CAST OF CANINE CHARACTERS

HAZELNUT

TEDDY

GINGER

COBBER

BILLIE

CHIPS

BOBBY

EDDIE

VIOLET

ROCKY

POPPY

MARRA

TOBY

COOPER

MONTY

JETT

ZAWADI

NZURI

ROXIE

DAKOTA

TILLY

NELSON

LULU

NOTES AND FURTHER READING

Chapter 1

Filiatre, J. C., J. L. Millot, and A. Eckerlin. 'Behavioural variability of olfactory exploration of the pet dog in relation to human adults.' *Applied Animal Behaviour Science* 30.3–4 (1991): 341–350.

Browne, C., K. Stafford, and R. Fordham. 'The use of scent-detection dogs.' *Irish Veterinary Journal* 59.2 (2006): 97.

Wackermannová, M., L. Pinc, and L. Jebavý. 'Olfactory Sensitivity in Mammalian Species.' *Physiological Research* 65.3 (2016): 369.

Edwards, Timothy L., et al. 'Animal olfactory detection of human diseases: Guidelines and systematic review.' *Journal of Veterinary Behavior: Clinical Applications and Research* (2017).

Warden, Carl John, and Lucien Hynes Warner. 'The sensory capacities and intelligence of dogs, with a report on the ability of the noted dog, Fellow, to respond to verbal stimuli.' *The Quarterly Review of Biology* 3.1 (1928): 1–28.

Bhadra, Anindita. 'Woof! Smells like cancer.' *Current Science* 101.4 (2011): 480–483.

Ninomiya, Yuzo, and Masaya Funakoshi. 'Responsiveness of dog thalamic neurons to taste stimulation of various tongue regions.' *Physiology & Behavior* 29.4 (1982): 741–745.

Chapter 2

Starling, Melissa J., et al. 'Canine sense and sensibility: tipping points and response latency variability as an optimism index in a canine judgement bias assessment.' *PLoS One* 9.9 (2014): e107794.

Burman, Oliver H. P., et al. 'Sensitivity to reward loss as an indicator of animal emotion and welfare.' *Biology Letters* 4.4 (2008): 330–333.

Christianson, John P., et al. 'Inhibition of fear by learned safety signals: a mini-symposium review.' *Journal of Neuroscience* 32.41 (2012): 14118–14124.

Kim, Hackjin, Shinsuke Shimojo, and John P. O'Doherty. 'Is avoiding an aversive outcome rewarding? Neural substrates of avoidance learning in the human brain.' *PLoS Biology* 4.8 (2006): e233.

Carver, Charles S., and Michael F. Scheier. 'Origins and functions of positive and negative affect: A control-process view.' *Psychological Review* 97.1 (1990): 19.

Rooney, Nicola J., and John W. S. Bradshaw. 'An experimental study of the effects of play upon the dog–human relationship.' *Applied Animal Behaviour Science* 75.2 (2002): 161–176.

Horowitz, Alexandra, and Julie Hecht. 'Examining dog–human play: the characteristics, affect, and vocalizations of a unique interspecific interaction.' *Animal Cognition* 19.4 (2016): 779–788.

Bálint, Anna, et al. '"Beware, I am big and non-dangerous!" Playfully growling dogs are perceived larger than their actual size by their canine audience.' *Applied Animal Behaviour Science* 148.1 (2013): 128–137.

Chapter 3

Yong, Min Hooi, and Ted Ruffman. 'Emotional contagion: Dogs and humans show a similar physiological response to human infant crying.' *Behavioural Processes* 108 (2014): 155–165.

Müller, C. A., et al. 'Dogs can discriminate emotional expressions of human faces.' *Current Biology* 25.5 (2015): 601–605.

Harris, Christine R., and Caroline Prouvost. 'Jealousy in dogs.' *PLoS One* 9.7 (2014): e94597.

Range, Friederike, et al. 'The absence of reward induces inequity aversion in dogs.' *Proceedings of the National Academy of Sciences* 106.1 (2009): 340–345.

Range, Friederike, Karin Leitner, and Zsófia Virányi. 'The influence of the relationship and motivation on inequity aversion in dogs.' *Social Justice Research* 25.2 (2012): 170–194.

Simonet, O., M. Murphy, and A. Lance. 'Laughing dog: Vocalizations of domestic dogs during play encounters.' *Animal Behavior Society Conference.* 2001.

Simonet, Patricia, Donna Versteeg, and Dan Storie. 'Dog-laughter: Recorded playback reduces stress related behavior in shelter dogs.' *Proceedings of the 7th International Conference on Environmental Enrichment.* Vol. 2005.

Raichlen, David A., et al. 'Wired to run: exercise-induced endocannabinoid signaling in humans and cursorial mammals with implications for the "runner's high".' *Journal of Experimental Biology* 215.8 (2012): 1331–1336.

Taylor, Anna M., David Reby, and Karen McComb. 'Context-related variation in the vocal growling behaviour of the domestic dog (*Canis familiaris*).' *Ethology* 115.10 (2009): 905–915.

McGreevy, Paul D., et al. 'An overview of the dog–human dyad and ethograms within it.' *Journal of Veterinary Behavior: Clinical Applications and Research* 7.2 (2012): 103–117.

McGreevy, Paul D., et al. 'Dog behavior co-varies with height, bodyweight and skull shape.' *PLoS One* 8.12 (2013): e80529.

Stone, Holly R., et al. 'Associations between domestic-dog morphology and behaviour scores in the Dog Mentality Assessment.' *PLoS One* 11.2 (2016): e0149403.

Chapter 4

Kron, Assaf, et al. 'Are valence and arousal separable in emotional experience?' *Emotion* 15.1 (2015): 35.

Mattek, A. M., G. L. Wolford, and P. J. Whalen. 'A mathematical model captures the structure of subjective affect.' *Perspectives on Psychological Science* 12.3 (2017): 508–526.

Reich, John W., and Alex J. Zautra. 'Arousal and the relationship between positive and negative affect: An analysis of the data of Ito, Cacioppo, and Lang (1998).' *Motivation and Emotion* 26.3 (2002): 209–222.

Beerda, Bonne, et al. 'Manifestations of chronic and acute stress in dogs.' *Applied Animal Behaviour Science* 52.3–4 (1997): 307–319.

Beerda, B., et al. 'Behavioural and hormonal indicators of enduring environmental stress in dogs.' *Animal Welfare Potters Bar* 9.1 (2000): 49–62.

Mariti, Chiara, et al. 'Perception of dogs' stress by their owners.' *Journal of Veterinary Behavior: Clinical Applications and Research* 7.4 (2012): 213–219.

Kerswell, Keven J., et al. 'Self-reported comprehension ratings of dog behavior by puppy owners.' *Anthrozoös* 22.2 (2009): 183–193.

Wan, Michele, Niall Bolger, and Frances A. Champagne. 'Human perception of fear in dogs varies according to experience with dogs.' *PLoS One* 7.12 (2012): e51775.

Firnkes, Angelika, et al. 'Appeasement signals used by dogs during dog–human communication.' *Journal of Veterinary Behavior: Clinical Applications and Research* 19 (2017): 35–44.

Chapter 5

Ong, Anthony D., et al. 'Psychological resilience, positive emotions, and successful adaptation to stress in later life.' *Journal of Personality and Social Psychology* 91.4 (2006): 730.

Peacock, E. J., and P. T. P. Wong. 'Anticipatory stress: The relation of locus of control, optimism, and control appraisals to coping.' *Journal of Research in Personality* 30.2 (1996): 204–222.

Lazarus, Richard S. 'Coping theory and research: Past, present, and future.' *Psychosomatic Medicine* 55.3 (1993): 234–247.

Starling, Melissa J., et al. 'Canine sense and sensibility: tipping points and response latency variability as an

optimism index in a canine judgement bias assessment.' *PLoS One* 9.9 (2014): e107794.

Roelofs, Sanne, et al. 'Making decisions under ambiguity: judgment bias tasks for assessing emotional state in animals.' *Frontiers in Behavioral Neuroscience* 10 (2016).

Mendl, Michael, Oliver H. P. Burman, and Elizabeth S. Paul. 'An integrative and functional framework for the study of animal emotion and mood.' *Proceedings of the Royal Society of London B: Biological Sciences* 277.1696 (2010): 2895–2904.

Burgdorf, Jeffrey, and Jaak Panksepp. 'The neurobiology of positive emotions.' *Neuroscience & Biobehavioral Reviews* 30.2 (2006): 173–187.

Chapter 6

Yerkes, Robert M., and John D. Dodson. 'The relation of strength of stimulus to rapidity of habit-formation.' *Journal of Comparative Neurology* 18.5 (1908): 459–482.

Hanoch, Yaniv, and Oliver Vitouch. 'When less is more: Information, emotional arousal and the ecological reframing of the Yerkes-Dodson law.' *Theory & Psychology* 14.4 (2004): 427–52.

Jing, Jian, Rhanor Gillette, and Klaudiusz R. Weiss. 'Evolving concepts of arousal: insights from simple model systems.' *Reviews in the Neurosciences* 20.5–6 (2009): 405–428.

Nicolaou, Mihalis A., Hatice Gunes, and Maja Pantic. 'Continuous prediction of spontaneous affect from multiple cues and modalities in valence-arousal space.' *IEEE Transactions on Affective Computing* 2.2 (2011): 92–105.

Chapter 7

Payne, E., et al. 'Evidence of horsemanship and dogmanship and their application in veterinary contexts.' *The Veterinary Journal Proceedings of the Royal Society*

B. Vol. 284. No. 1846. The Royal Society, 2017.204.3 (2015): 247–254.

Payne, Elyssa M., Pauleen C. Bennett, and Paul D. McGreevy. 'DogTube: An examination of dogmanship online.' *Journal of Veterinary Behavior: Clinical Applications and Research* 17 (2017): 50–61.

Payne, Elyssa M., et al. 'Dogmanship on the farm: Analysis of personality dimensions and training styles of stock dog handlers in Australia.' *Journal of Veterinary Behavior: Clinical Applications and Research* 10.6 (2015): 471–478.

McGreevy, Paul, et al. 'Defining and measuring dogmanship: A new multidisciplinary science to improve understanding of human–dog interactions.' *The Veterinary Journal* (2017).

Jeannin, Sarah, et al. 'Pet-directed speech draws adult dogs' attention more efficiently than adult-directed speech.' *Scientific Reports* 7.1 (2017): 4980.

Ben-Aderet, Tobey, et al. 'Dog-directed speech: why do we use it and do dogs pay attention to it?' *Proceedings of the Royal Society Series* B. Vol. 284. No. 1846. The Royal Society, 2017.

Ratcliffe, Victoria Frances. 'How dogs hear us: perception of the human voice by domestic dogs (*Canis familiaris*).' Dissertation. University of Sussex, 2016.

McConnell, Patricia B. 'Acoustic structure and receiver response in domestic dogs, *Canis familiaris*.' *Animal Behaviour* 39.5 (1990): 897–904.

Udell, Monique A. R., et al. 'Human-socialized wolves follow diverse human gestures… and they may not be alone.' *International Journal of Comparative Psychology* 25.2 (2012).

Browne, Clare Melody. 'The effects of delayed positive reinforcement on learning in dogs.' Dissertation. University of Waikato, 2015.

Fukuzawa, M., D. S. Mills, and J. J. Cooper. 'The effect of human command phonetic characteristics on auditory cognition in dogs (*Canis familiaris*).' *Journal of Comparative Psychology* 119.1 (2005): 117.

Arhant, Christine, et al. 'Behaviour of smaller and larger dogs: effects of training methods, inconsistency of owner behaviour and level of engagement in activities with the dog.' *Applied Animal Behaviour Science* 123.3 (2010): 131–142.

Horváth, Zsuzsánna, Antal Dóka, and Ádám Miklósi. 'Affiliative and disciplinary behavior of human handlers during play with their dog affects cortisol concentrations in opposite directions.' *Hormones and Behavior* 54.1 (2008): 107–114.

Faustino, Jillian. 'Pay attention! Can the type of interaction between handler and dog preceding an agility run affect a dog's attention during a run?' Undergraduate Review 7.1 (2011): 38–44.

Chapter 8

Gergely, Anna, et al. 'Dogs rapidly develop socially competent behaviour while interacting with a contingently responding self-propelled object.' *Animal Behaviour* 108 (2015): 137–144.

Bartholomew, K., & Horowitz, L. M. 'Attachment styles among young adults: A test of a four-category model.' *Journal of Personality and Social Psychology* 61(2) (1991): 226–244.

Horn, Lisa, Ludwig Huber, and Friederike Range. 'The importance of the secure base effect for domestic dogs–evidence from a manipulative problem-solving task.' *PLOS One* 8.5 (2013): e65296.

Palmer, Robyn, and Deborah Custance. 'A counterbalanced version of Ainsworth's Strange Situation Procedure reveals secure-base effects in dog–human relationships.' *Applied Animal Behaviour Science* 109.2 (2008): 306–319.

Kurdek, Lawrence A. 'Pet dogs as attachment figures.' Journal of Social and Personal Relationships 25.2 (2008):

247–266.

Zilcha-Mano, Sigal, Mario Mikulincer, and Phillip R. Shaver. 'Pets as safe havens and secure bases: The moderating role of pet attachment orientations.' *Journal of Research in Personality* 46.5 (2012): 571–580.

Payne, Elyssa, Pauleen C. Bennett, and Paul D. McGreevy. 'Current perspectives on attachment and bonding in the dog–human dyad.' *Psychology Research and Behavior Management* 8 (2015): 71.

Seksel, Kersti. 'Puppy socialization classes.' *Veterinary Clinics of North America: Small Animal Practice* 27.3 (1997): 465–477.

Howell, Tiffani J., and Pauleen C. Bennett. 'Puppy power! Using social cognition research tasks to improve socialization practices for domestic dogs (*Canis familiaris*).' *Journal of Veterinary Behavior: Clinical Applications and Research* 6.3 (2011): 195-204.

Freedman, Daniel G., John A. King, and Orville Elliot. 'Critical period in the social development of dogs.' *Science* 133.3457 (1961): 1016–1017.

Markwell, P. J., and C. J. Thorne. 'Early behavioural development of dogs.' *Journal of Small Animal Practice* 28.11 (1987): 984–991.

Daniels, Thomas J., and Marc Bekoff. 'Population and social biology of free-ranging dogs, *Canis familiaris*.' *Journal of Mammalogy* 70.4 (1989): 754–762.

Pal, S. K. 'Parental care in free-ranging dogs, *Canis familiaris*.' *Applied Animal Behaviour Science* 90.1 (2005): 31–47.

Bonanni, Roberto, et al. 'Free-ranging dogs assess the quantity of opponents in intergroup conflicts.' *Animal Cognition* 14.1 (2011): 103–115.

Pal, S. K., B. Ghosh, and S. Roy. 'Dispersal behaviour of free-ranging dogs (*Canis familiaris*) in relation to age, sex, season and dispersal distance.' *Applied Animal Behaviour Science* 61.2 (1998): 123–132.

Bonanni, R., et al. 'Effect of affiliative and agonistic relationships on leadership behaviour in free-ranging dogs.' *Animal Behaviour* 79.5 (2010): 981–991.

Boitani, Luigi, Paolo Ciucci, and Alessia Ortolani. 'Behaviour and social ecology of free-ranging dogs.' *The behavioural biology of dogs.* CAB International, Wallingford, UK, 2007. 147–165.

Majumder, Sreejani Sen, et al. 'To be or not to be social: foraging associations of free-ranging dogs in an urban eco-system.' *Acta Ethologica* 17.1 (2014): 1–8.

Bonanni, R., P. Valsecchi, and E. Natoli. 'Pattern of individual participation and cheating in conflicts between groups of free-ranging dogs.' *Animal Behaviour* 79.4 (2010): 957–968.

McCrave, Elizabeth A. 'Diagnostic criteria for separation anxiety in the dog.' *Veterinary Clinics of North America: Small Animal Practice* 21.2 (1991): 247-55.

Schilder, Matthijs B. H., Claudia M. Vinke, and Joanne A. M. van der Borg. 'Dominance in domestic dogs revisited: Useful habit and useful construct?' *Journal of Veterinary Behavior: Clinical Applications and Research* 9.4 (2014): 184–191.

van der Borg, Joanne A. M., et al. 'Dominance in domestic dogs: a quantitative analysis of its behavioural measures.' *PLOS One* 10.8 (2015): e0133978.

Trisko, Rebecca K., and Barbara B. Smuts. 'Dominance relationships in a group of domestic dogs (*Canis lupus familiaris*).' *Behaviour* 152.5 (2015): 677–704.

Chapter 9

Merola, Isabella, et al. 'Dogs' comprehension of referential emotional expressions: familiar people and familiar emotions are easier.' *Animal Cognition* 17.2 (2014): 373–385.

Buttelmann, David, and Michael Tomasello. "Can domestic dogs (Canis familiaris) use referential emotional

expressions to locate hidden food?."
Animal Cognition 16.1 (2013): 137–145.

Yong, Min Hooi, and Ted Ruffman. 'Is
that fear? Domestic dogs' use of social
referencing signals from an unfamiliar
person.' Behavioural Processes 110 (2015):
74–81.

Wallis, Lisa J., et al. 'Lifespan development
of attentiveness in domestic dogs:
drawing parallels with humans.'
Frontiers in psychology 5 (2014).

Wallis, Lisa J., et al. 'Aging effects on
discrimination learning, logical
reasoning and memory in pet
dogs.' Age 38.1 (2016): 6.

Chapagain, Durga, et al. 'Cognitive Aging
in Dogs.' Gerontology (2017).

Salvin, Hannah E., et al. 'The canine
cognitive dysfunction rating scale
(CCDR): a data-driven and ecologically
relevant assessment tool.'
The Veterinary Journal 188.3 (2011):
331–6.

Salvin, Hannah E., et al. 'Growing old
gracefully—Behavioral changes
associated with "successful aging" in the
dog, Canis familiaris.' Journal of
Veterinary Behavior: Clinical Applications
and Research 6.6 (2011): 313–320.

Yeates, James W. 'Is "a life worth living"
a concept worth having?' Animal
Welfare 20.3 (2011): 397–406.

Mellor, David J. 'Updating animal welfare
thinking: Moving beyond the "Five
Freedoms" towards "a Life Worth
Living".' Animals 6.3 (2016): 21.

Chapter 10

Starling, Melissa J., et al. 'Age, sex and
reproductive status affect boldness in
dogs.' The Veterinary Journal 197.3 (2013):
868–872.

Starling, Melissa J., et al. '"Boldness" in the
domestic dog differs among breeds and
breed groups.' Behavioural Processes 97
(2013): 53–62.

Turcsán, Borbála, Enik Kubinyi, and
Ádám Miklósi. 'Trainability and

boldness traits differ between dog breed
clusters based on conventional breed
categories and genetic relatedness.'
Applied Animal Behaviour Science 132.1
(2011): 61–70.

Fratkin, Jamie L., et al. 'Personality
consistency in dogs: a meta-
analysis.' PLOS One 8.1 (2013): e54907.

Rayment, Diana J., et al. 'Applied
personality assessment in domestic
dogs: Limitations and caveats.' Applied
Animal Behaviour Science 163 (2015): 1-18.

Riemer, Stefanie, et al. 'The predictive
value of early behavioural assessments
in pet dogs–A longitudinal study from
neonates to adults.' PLoS One 9.7 (2014):
e101237.

Riemer, Stefanie, Daniel S. Mills, and
Hannah Wright. 'Impulsive for life? The
nature of long-term impulsivity in
domestic dogs.' Animal Cognition 17.3
(2014): 815–819.

Sherman, Barbara L., et al. 'A test for the
evaluation of emotional reactivity in
Labrador retrievers used for explosives
detection.' Journal of Veterinary
Behavior: Clinical Applications and
Research 10.2 (2015): 94–102.

McGarrity, Monica E., David L. Sinn, and
Samuel D. Gosling. 'Which personality
dimensions do puppy tests measure? A
systematic procedure for categorizing
behavioral assays.' Behavioural
Processes 110 (2015): 117–124.

Wright, Hannah F., Daniel S. Mills, and
Petra M. J. Pollux. 'Behavioural and
physiological correlates of impulsivity
in the domestic dog (Canis familiaris).'
Physiology & Behavior 105.3 (2012):
676–82.

Wright, Hannah F., et al. 'Development
and Validation of a Psychometric Tool
for Assessing Impulsivity in the
Domestic Dog (Canis familiaris).'
International Journal of Comparative
Psychology 24.2 (2011).

Koolhaas, J. M., et al. 'Coping styles in
animals: current status in behavior and

stress-physiology.' Neuroscience &
Biobehavioral Reviews 23.7 (1999):
925–35.

Coppens, Caroline M., Sietse F. de Boer,
and Jaap M. Koolhaas. 'Coping styles
and behavioural flexibility: towards
underlying mechanisms.' Philosophical
Transactions of the Royal Society of
London B: Biological Sciences 365.1560
(2010): 4021–8.

Francis, Darlene, et al. 'Nongenomic
transmission across generations of
maternal behavior and stress responses
in the rat.' Science 286.5442 (1999):
1155–8.

McMillan, Franklin D., et al. Differences
in behavioral characteristics between
dogs obtained as puppies from pet stores
and those obtained from non-
commercial breeders.' Journal of the
American Veterinary Medical
Association 242.10 (2013): 1359–63.

Nicholas, Frank W., Elizabeth R. Arnott,
and Paul D. McGreevy. 'Hybrid vigour
in dogs?' The Veterinary Journal 214
(2016): 77–83.

O'Neill, D. G., et al. ;Longevity and
mortality of owned dogs in England.;
The Veterinary Journal 198.3 (2013):
638–643.

Dan, G. O., et al. 'Prevalence of disorders
recorded in dogs attending primary-
care veterinary practices in
England.' PLoS One 9.3 (2014): e90501.

The Smart Puppy and Dog Buyer's Guide,
RSPCA and RSPCA Australia.

INDEX

Published in 2018 by Murdoch Books, an imprint of Allen & Unwin

Murdoch Books Australia
83 Alexander Street,
Crows Nest NSW 2065
Phone: +61 (0)2 8425 0100
murdochbooks.com.au
info@murdochbooks.com.au

Murdoch Books UK
Ormond House, 26–27 Boswell Street,
London, WC1N 3JZ
Phone: +44 (0) 20 8785 5995
murdochbooks.co.uk
info@murdochbooks.co.uk

For Corporate Orders & Custom Publishing contact our business
development team at salesenquiries@murdochbooks.com.au

Publisher: Jane Morrow
Editor: Jane Price
Designer: Madeleine Kane
Photography: Cath Muscat
Production Manager: Lou Playfair
(Cover image Shutterstock: Richard Chaff)

Text © Melissa Starling and Paul McGreevy
Design © Murdoch Books 2018
Photography © Cath Muscat

ISBN 978 1 76063 122 2 Australia
ISBN 978 1 76063 404 9 UK

A cataloguing-in-publication entry is available from the catalogue
of the National Library of Australia at nla.gov.au
A catalogue record for this book is available from the British Library

Colour reproduction by Splitting Image Colour Studio Pty Ltd, Clayton, Victoria
Printed by 1010 Printing, China